Pawsitive Training

A Comprehensive Guide to Positive Dog Training and Techniques for Happy and Confident Dogs, Including Those with Reactive Behavior

By

Laurel Marsh

© **Copyright 2024 by Laurel Marsh- All rights reserved.**

This document is geared towards providing exact and reliable information with regards to the topic and issue covered. The publication is sold with the idea that the publisher is not required to render accounting, officially permitted, or otherwise, qualified services. If advice is necessary, legal or professional, a practiced individual in the profession should be ordered. From a Declaration of Principles which was accepted and approved equally by a Committee of the American Bar Association and a Committee of Publishers and Associations. In no way is it legal to reproduce, duplicate, or transmit any part of this document in either electronic means or in printed format. Recording of this publication is strictly prohibited and any storage of this document is not allowed unless with written permission from the publisher.

All rights reserved.

The information provided herein is stated to be truthful and consistent, in that any liability, in terms of inattention or otherwise, by any usage or abuse of any policies, processes, or directions contained within is the solitary and utter responsibility of the recipient reader. Under no circumstances will any legal responsibility or blame be held against the publisher for any reparation, damages, or monetary loss due to the information herein, either directly or indirectly. Respective authors own all copyrights not held by the publisher. The information herein is offered for informational purposes solely, and is universal as so. The presentation of the information is without contract or any type of guarantee assurance. The trademarks that are used are without any consent, and the publication of the trademark is without permission or backing by the trademark owner. All trademarks and brands within this book are for clarifying purposes only and are the owned by the owners themselves, not affiliated with this document.

Dear reader,

As an author deeply immersed in the world of dog sitting, I have poured my heart and soul into crafting this comprehensive guide to positive dog training. My journey began with a profound love for animals, particularly dogs, whose unwavering companionship and boundless joy enrich our lives in countless ways.

Throughout my career as a seasoned dog sitter, I have dedicated myself to providing a nurturing environment for our furry friends. Each day, I am privileged to witness the wagging tails and wet noses that signify the profound bond between humans and dogs. It is this connection that has fueled my passion for understanding canine behavior and developing effective training techniques.

In writing this book, I have drawn upon years of experience and expertise to offer practical advice and valuable insights into the world of positive dog training. My goal is to empower fellow dog lovers with the knowledge and tools they need to cultivate harmonious relationships with their canine companions.

As an independent author, I understand the significance of reader feedback and support. Reviews on platforms like Amazon not only provide valuable insights for potential readers but also play a crucial role in supporting authors like myself. Your honest feedback and reviews are invaluable, shaping the future of my work and helping to spread the message of positive dog training far and wide.

I am deeply grateful for the opportunity to share my passion for dogs and positive training techniques with you. Together, let us embark on a journey to nurture happier, healthier relationships with our beloved canine friends.

Warm regards,

Laurel Marsh

Table of Contents

Introduction 7

Chapter 1: The Foundations of Positive Dog Training 8
   1.1 Understanding the Benefits of Positive Training 8
   1.2 Exploring the Power of Positive Reinforcement 10
   1.3 Debunking Common Myths about Aggression and Reactivity 11
   1.4 Addressing Behavioral Issues with Positive Methods 12
   1.5 Strengthening the Bond Between Dog and Owner 13
   1.6 Indoor & Outdoor Fun Games 15

Chapter 2: Understanding Canine Behavior 26
   2.1 Exploring Canine Psychology 26
   2.2 Recognizing Reactive and Aggressive Behaviors 28
   2.3 Exploring Different Types of Canine Aggression 28
   2.4 Considering the Role of Breed in Behavior 31
   2.5 Interpreting Your Dog's Body Language 32
   2.6 Nurturing Well-Rounded Puppies through Positive Socialization 33

Chapter 3: Training Principles and Techniques 36
   3.1 The Fundamentals of Dog Training 36
   3.2 Different Types of Dog Training 37
   3.3 Tailoring Training Approaches to Your Dog's Breed and Personality 43
   3.4 Avoiding Common Training Mistakes 44

Chapter 4: Tailored Training Programs 46
   4.1 Designing Training Programs for Pets of All Ages 46
   4.2 Addressing Specific Training Needs for Older Dogs 46
   4.3 Implementing Effective Training Strategies for Rescue Dogs 48
   4.4 Case Studies 50
   4.5 Providing Recommended Reading, Websites, and Training Tools 52

Chapter 5: Health and Wellness 56
   5.1 Prioritizing Nutrition for Optimal Health 56
   5.2 Identifying Safe and Unsafe Foods for Dogs 57
   5.3 Nutritious Recipes for Homemade Dog Meals 59
   1. Chicken and Sweet Potato Stew 60
   2. Beef and Barley Casserole 60
   3. Turkey and Rice Pilaf 61
   4. Salmon and Quinoa Salad 61

- 5. Lamb and Vegetable Stir-Fry 62
- 6. Tuna and Brown Rice Bowl 62
- 7. Pork and Pumpkin Chili 63
- 8. Venison and Lentil Soup 64
- 9. Duck and Potato Hash 64
- 10. Cod and Spinach Bake 65
- 11. Rabbit and Carrot Stew 65
- 12. Sardine and Oatmeal Porridge 66
- 13. Trout and Carrot Mash 66
- 14. Beef and Spinach Lasagna 67
- 13. Trout and Carrot Mash 67
- 15. Pork and Apple Stew 68
- 13. Trout and Carrot Mash 68
- 16. Turkey and Cranberry Meatballs 69
- 17. Salmon and Pumpkin Pasta 69
- 18. Duck and Blueberry Bake 70
- 19. Chicken and Chickpea Curry 70
- 20. Trout and Couscous Salad 71
- 5.4 Canine First Aid: Basic Emergency Care for Dogs 72
- 72
- 1. Identifying Common Health Emergencies 72

Chapter 6: Advanced Training and Enrichment 84
- 6.1 Advancing Beyond Basic Training: Competition, Working, and Therapy Dog Training 84
- 6.2 Enhancing Communication and Understanding Between Owner and Dog 87
- 6.3 Managing Time Effectively for Training Sessions 89

Dog IQ Test: Assessing Canine Intelligence 91

Conclusion 93

BONUS 1 94

HERBAL REMEDIES FOR PETS 94

BONUS 2 95

MUSIC FOR DOG 95

Introduction

All of us adore our dogs, but how many times have they driven us to the brink of exasperation? How often have we felt overwhelmed by their behaviors, wishing we could provide them with the right guidance and training?

Welcome to "Positive Training For Reactive Dogs," a guide born from a shared understanding of the challenges dog owners face and a deep-seated love for our canine companions. As someone who has experienced firsthand the trials and triumphs of navigating life with reactive dogs, I understand the frustrations and uncertainties that can accompany this journey.

In this book, we embark on a transformative exploration of positive dog training, recognizing the unique needs and sensitivities of reactive dogs. With compassion and empathy, we delve into the world of positive reinforcement, seeking to unravel the complexities of canine behavior and forge a path towards harmony and understanding.

Our journey begins with a recognition of the profound bond between humans and dogs, acknowledging the quirks and idiosyncrasies that make each dog a cherished member of our families. While our dogs may test our patience at times, their unwavering loyalty and unconditional love remind us of the profound connection we share.

Throughout these pages, we'll delve into practical techniques and strategies designed to empower you as a dog owner, equipping you with the knowledge and skills necessary to address reactive behaviors with patience and compassion. From understanding the benefits of positive training methods to tailoring approaches to your dog's unique personality, our aim is to guide you towards a deeper understanding of your canine companion and foster a relationship built on trust and mutual respect. Moreover, as a special bonus, we've included an IQ test to uncover your dog's intelligence and fun indoor and outdoor games to keep both you and your furry friend entertained and engaged.

But this book is more than just a training manual; it's a testament to the transformative power of love and dedication. It's a beacon of hope for every dog owner seeking to unlock the full potential of their beloved pet. With dedication, patience, and a commitment to positive reinforcement, we can overcome any challenge and build a brighter future for our furry friends. With each page turned and each lesson learned, we move closer towards a future where every dog has the opportunity to thrive in a supportive and nurturing environment.

Chapter 1: The Foundations of Positive Dog Training

In this foundational chapter, we lay the groundwork for our journey into the world of positive dog training. We'll explore the transformative power of positive reinforcement, debunk common myths surrounding canine behavior, and delve into practical techniques for addressing behavioral issues with compassion and empathy. Our aim is to equip you with the knowledge and skills necessary to build a strong bond with your dog based on trust, respect, and mutual understanding.

1.1 Understanding the Benefits of Positive Training

Positive training methods have gained widespread recognition for their effectiveness in fostering a harmonious relationship between dogs and their owners. Unlike punitive methods that rely on fear and intimidation, positive training focuses on rewarding desired behaviors, encouraging dogs to learn and cooperate willingly.

1. Enhanced Learning and Cooperation. Positive reinforcement taps into a dog's natural inclination to seek rewards, making learning a positive and enjoyable experience. By rewarding desired behaviors such as sitting, staying, and coming when called, dogs are motivated to repeat these behaviors in anticipation of praise, treats, or other rewards.

2. Strengthened Bond Between Dog and Owner. Positive training strengthens the bond between dog and owner by fostering trust, mutual respect, and clear communication. By focusing on positive interactions and rewards, dogs learn to associate their owners with pleasure and fulfillment, deepening the emotional connection between them.

3. Reduced Stress and Anxiety. Punitive training methods can cause stress, anxiety, and even aggression in dogs, leading to behavioral issues and strained relationships. In contrast, positive training creates a supportive and nurturing environment where dogs feel safe to explore, learn, and express themselves freely.

4. Long-Term Behavior Modification. Positive training methods focus on addressing the root causes of behavioral issues rather than simply suppressing unwanted behaviors through punishment. By identifying and rewarding desirable behaviors while gently redirecting or managing undesirable ones, positive training promotes long-term behavior modification and helps dogs develop self-control and impulse management skills.

5. Adaptability to Different Dogs and Situations. Positive training techniques are highly adaptable and can be tailored to suit the individual needs, personalities, and learning styles of different dogs. Whether you're training a playful puppy, a mature dog, or a rescued companion with a troubled past, positive training offers a flexible and compassionate approach that empowers dogs to thrive in any situation.

6. Improved Problem-Solving Skills. Positive training encourages dogs to think and problem-solve, as they actively seek out behaviors that result in rewards. This mental stimulation not only enhances their cognitive abilities but also promotes a sense of fulfillment and confidence.

7. Reduced Risk of Aggression. Positive training methods promote a calm and respectful relationship between dogs and their owners, reducing the likelihood of fear-based aggression or defensive behaviors. By focusing on positive interactions and clear communication, positive training fosters trust and security in dogs, minimizing the risk of conflicts or confrontations.

8. Enhanced Socialization. Positive training provides opportunities for dogs to interact with other dogs and people in a positive and controlled manner. This promotes socialization skills and helps dogs develop confidence and resilience in various social settings, reducing the risk of fear or anxiety-related behaviors in unfamiliar situations.

9. Greater Flexibility in Training. Positive training techniques offer a wide range of tools and methods that can be tailored to suit the specific needs and preferences of both dogs and owners. From clicker training to shaping behaviors through luring and capturing, positive training provides a flexible and adaptable approach that empowers owners to achieve their training goals effectively.

10. Increased Enjoyment for Both Dog and Owner. Perhaps one of the most significant benefits of positive training is the sheer enjoyment it brings to both dogs and their owners. By focusing on positive interactions, rewards, and mutual respect, positive training transforms the training process into a fun and fulfilling experience for everyone involved, strengthening the bond between dog and owner in the process.

In summary, the benefits of positive training extend far beyond obedience commands and behavioral corrections. By fostering a relationship based on trust, respect, and mutual understanding, positive training transforms the lives of dogs and their owners, paving the way for a lifetime of companionship, joy, and mutual enrichment.

1.2 Exploring the Power of Positive Reinforcement

Positive reinforcement stands as a pivotal pillar in the realm of effective dog training, leveraging the inherent desire of our canine companions to seek out rewards and using these rewards strategically to reinforce desired behaviors. At its essence, positive reinforcement involves the rewarding of behaviors we wish to encourage, thereby increasing the likelihood of their recurrence in the future. This reinforcement can manifest in various forms, from tasty treats and enthusiastic praise to coveted toys or even a simple pat on the head, all tailored to what the individual dog finds most rewarding. The timing and consistency of these rewards play a fundamental role in the efficacy of positive reinforcement. It's imperative that rewards are delivered promptly following the desired behavior, allowing the dog to make a clear connection between their actions and the subsequent reward. Consistency in reinforcement is equally vital, as it helps dogs understand what is expected of them and reinforces the reliability of their actions. Erratic or unpredictable reinforcement can lead to confusion and inconsistency in behavior, hindering the training process.

Positive reinforcement also embraces the concepts of shaping and capturing behaviors, allowing trainers to guide dogs towards desired behaviors gradually. Shaping involves breaking down complex behaviors into manageable steps and rewarding each incremental progression towards the desired behavior. This method enables dogs to learn at their own pace, building upon their existing skills while reinforcing their successes along the way. Additionally, positive reinforcement can capitalize on spontaneous behaviors that dogs naturally exhibit, capturing these behaviors and incorporating them into the training repertoire. Crucially, positive reinforcement eschews punitive measures in favor of reinforcing desired behaviors. Punishment-based methods can instill fear, anxiety, and even aggression in dogs, undermining the trust and bond between dog and owner. By focusing on positive reinforcement, trainers create a supportive and nurturing training environment where dogs feel safe to explore, learn, and express themselves freely. Beyond the immediate training benefits, positive reinforcement nurtures confidence and trust in dogs, empowering them to engage in training exercises with enthusiasm and a willingness to participate. This fosters a strong bond between dog and owner, built on mutual respect and understanding. Moreover, positive reinforcement promotes long-term behavior modification by addressing the underlying motivations and emotions driving a dog's behavior. By rewarding desired behaviors and providing appropriate outlets for their natural instincts, positive reinforcement cultivates self-control, impulse management, and social skills that endure beyond the training sessions.

In essence, the power of positive reinforcement lies in its ability to tap into the intrinsic motivations and desires of dogs, fostering a positive and rewarding learning experience for both dog and owner. By embracing positive reinforcement techniques, trainers unlock the full potential of their canine companions, nurturing a relationship characterized by trust, respect, and mutual enrichment.

1.3 Debunking Common Myths about Aggression and Reactivity

Within the realm of dog behavior, myths and misconceptions often abound, particularly regarding aggression and reactivity. In this section, we'll try to dispel these myths and shed light on the complex nature of aggression and reactivity in dogs.

1. Aggression Equals Dominance. One prevailing myth suggests that aggressive behavior in dogs stems from a desire to assert dominance over their owners or other dogs. However, contemporary research suggests that aggression is rarely driven by a desire for dominance and is more often a response to fear, anxiety, or insecurity. Dogs may exhibit aggressive behaviors as a means of self-defense or as a reaction to perceived threats, rather than a deliberate attempt to establish dominance.

2. Breed Determines Behavior. Another common misconception revolves around the idea that a dog's breed dictates its behavior, particularly when it comes to aggression. While certain breeds may have predispositions towards certain behaviors, such as herding or retrieving, aggression is not inherently linked to breed. Aggression and reactivity can manifest in dogs of any breed, and factors such as socialization, training, and individual temperament play significant roles in shaping a dog's behavior.

3. Aggression is Unpredictable. Many people believe that aggressive behavior in dogs is unpredictable and uncontrollable, leading to fear and mistrust of certain breeds or individual dogs. In reality, aggression is often predictable and can be influenced by various environmental, genetic, and social factors. By understanding the triggers and warning signs of aggression, dog owners can take proactive measures to prevent or manage aggressive incidents effectively.

4. Punishment is the Solution. There is a common misconception that punitive methods are the most effective way to address aggression in dogs, with some advocating for harsh disciplinary measures to suppress aggressive behaviors. However, punishment-based methods can exacerbate aggression, leading to increased fear, anxiety, and defensive reactions in dogs. Positive, reward-based training methods offer a more humane and effective approach to addressing aggression, focusing on reinforcing desired behaviors and building trust and confidence in dogs.

5. Reactive Dogs are Beyond Help. Many dog owners believe that reactive dogs are beyond help and resign themselves to managing their dog's reactive behaviors rather than addressing them directly. However, with patience, consistency, and appropriate training techniques, most reactive behaviors can be modified and managed effectively. By understanding the underlying triggers and employing positive training methods, owners can help their reactive dogs overcome their reactivity and lead fulfilling lives.

6. Aggression is Inherited. There's a misconception that aggressive behavior in dogs is solely determined by genetics and that dogs with aggressive parents will inevitably display aggressive tendencies themselves. While genetics can influence temperament to some extent, environment, upbringing, and socialization play equally significant roles in shaping a dog's behavior. Responsible breeding practices and early socialization can mitigate the risk of aggression in dogs, regardless of their genetic predispositions.

7. Neutering Eliminates Aggression. Some people believe that neutering or spaying a dog will automatically eliminate aggressive tendencies, particularly in male dogs. While neutering can reduce certain types of aggression related to mating behaviors, it is not a guaranteed solution for all forms of aggression. Aggression in dogs is multifaceted and can stem from various underlying factors, including fear, anxiety, and territoriality. Neutering should be viewed as one component of a comprehensive behavior management plan, rather than a standalone solution.

8. Aggressive Dogs Cannot Be Rehabilitated. There's a pervasive belief that once a dog displays aggressive behavior, they are beyond rehabilitation and destined to remain aggressive for life. In reality, many aggressive behaviors can be modified and managed through proper training, behavior modification techniques, and environmental management. With patience, consistency, and the guidance of qualified professionals, even severely aggressive dogs can learn to exhibit more appropriate behaviors and lead fulfilling lives.

9. Aggression is Always Obvious. Contrary to popular belief, aggression in dogs is not always overt or easily recognizable. While some dogs may exhibit growling, snarling, or snapping when they feel threatened or fearful, others may display more subtle signs of aggression, such as lip licking, whale eye, or freezing in place. Recognizing these subtle cues is crucial for understanding a dog's emotional state and addressing potential aggression before it escalates.

10. Aggression is a Sign of a Bad Dog. Finally, there's a pervasive myth that aggressive behavior in dogs is indicative of a "bad" or inherently aggressive dog. In reality, aggression is a complex behavior influenced by a myriad of factors, including genetics, environment, past experiences, and socialization. Labeling a dog as "bad" based on their aggressive behavior oversimplifies the issue and overlooks the underlying reasons behind the behavior. With proper understanding, training, and support, most dogs can overcome aggression and thrive in loving, supportive environments.

By debunking these common myths about aggression and reactivity, we pave the way for a deeper understanding of canine behavior and promote more compassionate and effective approaches to training and behavior management. Through education and awareness, we empower dog owners to recognize the signs of aggression and reactivity, address them proactively, and build stronger, more harmonious relationships with their canine companions.

1.4 Addressing Behavioral Issues with Positive Methods

In this section, we delve into the effective application of positive training methods to address a wide range of behavioral issues in dogs. Rather than resorting to punitive measures or outdated training techniques, positive methods emphasize the importance of understanding the root causes of behavioral issues and implementing strategies that promote trust, confidence, and cooperation between dogs and their owners.

1. Understanding the Underlying Causes. The first step in addressing behavioral issues with positive methods is to identify and understand the underlying causes of the problematic behaviors. Whether it's excessive barking, destructive chewing, or separation anxiety, behavioral issues often stem from factors such as fear, anxiety, boredom, or lack of socialization.

By pinpointing the root cause of the behavior, trainers can develop targeted intervention strategies that address the underlying motivations driving the behavior.

2. Positive Reinforcement and Desensitization. Positive reinforcement lies at the heart of addressing behavioral issues, rewarding desired behaviors and reinforcing alternative, more appropriate behaviors. By using rewards such as treats, praise, or play to encourage positive behaviors, trainers can effectively shape and modify a dog's behavior over time. Additionally, desensitization techniques can help dogs overcome fears or anxieties by gradually exposing them to the trigger in a controlled and positive manner, rewarding calm and relaxed behavior.

3. Counterconditioning. Counterconditioning involves pairing the presence of a perceived threat or trigger with a positive experience to change the dog's emotional response to that stimulus. For example, if a dog displays fear or aggression towards strangers, counterconditioning techniques may involve associating the presence of strangers with treats, praise, or play, gradually helping the dog develop a positive association with unfamiliar people.

4. Environmental Management. In addition to training techniques, environmental management plays a crucial role in addressing behavioral issues. This may involve modifying the dog's environment to reduce stressors or triggers, providing ample mental and physical stimulation to prevent boredom, and establishing consistent routines and boundaries to promote a sense of security and predictability for the dog.

5. Patience and Consistency. Addressing behavioral issues with positive methods requires patience, consistency, and commitment from both the owner and the trainer. Rome wasn't built in a day, and neither are behavior modification efforts. It's essential to set realistic expectations, celebrate small victories, and remain consistent in implementing positive reinforcement techniques to achieve long-term behavioral changes.

6. Seeking Professional Guidance. In some cases, addressing complex behavioral issues may require the expertise of a qualified professional, such as a certified dog trainer or behaviorist. These professionals can conduct a thorough assessment of the dog's behavior, develop a tailored behavior modification plan, and provide guidance and support to both the owner and the dog throughout the training process.

1.5 Strengthening the Bond Between Dog and Owner

The bond between a dog and its owner is truly special, transcending mere companionship to become a profound connection built on shared experiences, mutual understanding, and unconditional love. Spending quality time together is crucial for fortifying this bond. Whether it's embarking on long walks, playing fetch in the park, or simply cuddling on the couch, these shared moments create enduring memories and deepen the bond between you and your furry friend. Effective communication forms the bedrock of this relationship. Learning to decipher your dog's body language and vocal cues enables you to respond adeptly to their needs and emotions, thereby strengthening the bond of trust between you. Trust and respect constitute fundamental pillars of any strong relationship. By consistently employing positive reinforcement and eschewing punishment-based methods, you demonstrate to your dog that you are a reliable and trustworthy leader upon whom they can depend.

Engaging in novel experiences together further solidifies the bond between you and your dog. Whether it's exploring a new hiking trail or participating in a dog-friendly event, these shared adventures forge lasting memories and deepen your connection. Moreover, consistency and patience play pivotal roles in establishing and reinforcing this bond. Consistency in enforcing rules and responding predictably to your dog's behaviors fosters a sense of structure and security, contributing to bond reinforcement. Patience is equally vital during the bonding process, as overcoming challenges or difficulties may necessitate time and dedication. Additionally, it's imperative to acknowledge the emotional fulfillment derived from a robust and positive bond with your dog. This bond enriches both your lives, offering companionship, solace, and joy in everyday experiences.

Building Trust Through Positive Interactions

Trust serves as the cornerstone of any robust relationship, and nurturing it with your canine companion is essential for fostering a harmonious bond. Positive interactions play a pivotal role in cultivating trust between you and your dog, spanning a broad spectrum of activities ranging from basic training exercises to everyday interactions such as playtime, grooming, and feeding. Each interaction presents an opportunity to bolster trust and deepen your bond. As we said before, consistency is paramount in building trust through positive interactions. By consistently providing positive experiences and responses, you establish a sense of reliability and predictability that your dog can rely on. This consistency engenders feelings of security and confidence in your relationship, laying the groundwork for a robust and enduring bond. Positive reinforcement serves as another potent tool in building trust with your dog. By rewarding desired behaviors with praise, treats, or other incentives, you foster positive associations and incentivize your dog to repeat these behaviors in the future. This constructive feedback reinforces your dog's trust in you as a source of guidance and support. Effective communication forms an essential component of trust-building. Paying heed to your dog's body language and vocalizations and responding appropriately to their cues and signals engenders empathy and sensitivity, crucial ingredients for trust-building. Activities geared towards building trust, such as training exercises and interactive games, offer invaluable opportunities for bonding and reinforcement. Engage in activities that challenge your dog both mentally and physically, instilling a sense of achievement and fulfillment that strengthens your bond. Patience and understanding are indispensable throughout the trust-building process, as trust takes time to cultivate and necessitates unwavering commitment and dedication.

Trust-building activities, such as training exercises and interactive games, provide valuable opportunities for bonding and reinforcement. Engage in activities that challenge your dog mentally and physically, fostering a sense of accomplishment and fulfillment that strengthens your bond. Patience and understanding are essential throughout the trust-building process. Trust takes time to develop and requires patience, consistency, and dedication.

Developing Impulse Control and Frustration Tolerance

Impulse control denotes the capacity to resist immediate impulses or urges in favor of more desirable behavior. Dogs, akin to humans, grapple with impulses to engage in certain behaviors, be it chasing a squirrel, leaping on visitors, or snatching food from the table.

Cultivating impulse control empowers dogs to regulate their behavior and make judicious choices in diverse situations. Frustration tolerance, conversely, entails the ability to cope with frustration or disappointment when circumstances diverge from expectations. Dogs, akin to humans, may experience frustration upon encountering obstacles or challenges, such as being unable to access a coveted toy or treat. Developing frustration tolerance equips dogs with the tools to maintain composure and equanimity in trying situations, rather than succumbing to agitation or reactivity. Fostering impulse control and frustration tolerance in dogs necessitates patience, consistency, and positive reinforcement. Training exercises centered on impulse control, such as "leave it" or "stay," aid dogs in resisting temptation and exercising self-restraint. Similarly, teaching dogs to await their meals or attention patiently fosters patience and tolerance for deferred gratification. Initiating the development of impulse control and frustration tolerance in dogs from a tender age is imperative, as these skills require time to mature and strengthen. Consistent training and reinforcement are pivotal to success, alongside establishing clear behavioral expectations and boundaries. In tandem with training exercises, providing enrichment activities and mental stimulation enables dogs to channel their energy and focus productively. Interactive toys, puzzle feeders, and training games furnish opportunities for dogs to engage their minds and practice impulse control in a gratifying and enjoyable manner. Ultimately, fostering impulse control and frustration tolerance not only ameliorates dogs' behavior but also fortifies the bond between dogs and their owners. By empowering dogs to regulate their impulses and cope with frustration constructively, we facilitate better decision-making and bolster dogs' confidence and adaptability. This, in turn, engenders a deeper sense of trust and understanding between dogs and their owners, laying the groundwork for a resilient and enduring bond.

1.6 Indoor & Outdoor Fun Games

This section offers a variety of engaging activities to keep your dog entertained, mentally stimulated, and physically active, regardless of the weather or space constraints. Whether you're playing indoors to beat the heat or rain, or enjoying the great outdoors on a sunny day, these games provide opportunities for bonding, training, and fun-filled interaction between you and your furry companion. From interactive puzzles to agility training, there's something for every dog's preference and energy level. Let's explore each activity in detail to ensure a rewarding experience for both you and your dog.

INDOOR FUN GAMES

1. DIY Obstacle Course with Cardboard Boxes

- ✓ **Description**: Create an obstacle course using cardboard boxes, tunnels, and other household items. Design challenges like crawling under tables, jumping over hurdles, or weaving through cones.
- ✓ **Tips**: Ensure boxes are secure and safe for your dog to navigate. Start with simple obstacles and gradually increase difficulty. Use treats or toys as incentives to complete the course.
- ✓ **Benefits**: Promotes physical exercise, mental stimulation, and problem-solving skills.

2. Interactive Feeding Toys or Treat Dispensers

- ✓ **Description**: Use interactive toys that dispense treats or kibble as your dog plays with them. These toys engage your dog's natural foraging instincts and provide mental stimulation.
- ✓ **Tips**: Choose toys suitable for your dog's size and chewing habits. Supervise your dog during play to prevent ingestion of non-edible parts. Rotate toys regularly to keep your dog engaged.
- ✓ **Benefits**: Encourages independent play, reduces boredom and anxiety, and slows down eating for dogs prone to gulping.

3. Shadow Chasing Games

- ✓ **Description**: Use a flashlight to create moving shadows on the wall or floor, and let your dog chase them. This game mimics hunting behavior and provides a fun and interactive way to burn off excess energy.
- ✓ **Tips**: Avoid shining the light directly into your dog's eyes. Start with slow, gentle movements to prevent overexcitement. End the game if your dog becomes too aroused.
- ✓ **Benefits**: Provides mental and physical stimulation, strengthens the bond between you and your dog, and offers an outlet for predatory instincts.

4. Playing with a Laser Pointer (with Caution)

- ✓ **Description:** Use a laser pointer to create a moving light spot for your dog to chase. This game can be entertaining for dogs with a strong prey drive.
- ✓ **Tips:** Avoid shining the laser directly into your dog's eyes to prevent eye damage. Limit sessions to short bursts to prevent frustration. Always follow up with a tangible toy or treat to provide closure
- ✓ **Benefits:** Offers mental stimulation, encourages physical activity, and provides an outlet for chasing instincts.

5. Staircase Training for Agility and Exercise

- ✓ **Description:** Utilize your staircase for agility exercises such as climbing up and down, weaving between steps, or practicing jumps.
- ✓ **Tips:** Start with small steps and gradually increase difficulty. Use treats or toys as motivation. Ensure your dog is physically capable and supervise closely to prevent accidents.
- ✓ **Benefits:** Builds strength and endurance, improves coordination and balance, and provides mental stimulation through learning new skills.

6. Hide and Seek

- ✓ **Description:** Hide somewhere in your home and call your dog's name. Encourage them to find you by using verbal cues or calling their attention.
- ✓ **Tips:** Start with easy hiding spots and gradually increase difficulty. Use treats or toys to reward your dog when they find you. Keep sessions short and positive.
- ✓ **Benefits:** Enhances recall skills, strengthens the bond between you and your dog, and provides mental stimulation through problem-solving.

7. Scent Work or Nose Games

- ✓ **Description:** Hide treats or toys around your home and encourage your dog to find them using their sense of smell. You can gradually increase difficulty by hiding items in more challenging locations.
- ✓ **Tips:** Start with easy hiding spots and gradually increase difficulty. Use high-value treats or toys to maintain your dog's interest. Keep sessions short to prevent frustration.
- ✓ **Benefits:** Stimulates your dog's sense of smell, provides mental enrichment, and offers a rewarding activity for dogs of all ages.

8. Tug of War

- ✓ **Description:** Engage in a game of tug with your dog using a sturdy rope toy or tugger. Let your dog grab one end of the toy and pull while you gently resist.
- ✓ **Tips:** Establish rules to prevent rough play and maintain control of the game. Use a designated tug toy to prevent your dog from associating other items with tug play. End the game if your dog becomes overly excited or aggressive.
- ✓ **Benefits:** Builds jaw strength and muscle tone, provides mental and physical exercise, and strengthens the bond between you and your dog through interactive play.

9. Trick Training Sessions

- ✓ **Description:** Teach your dog new tricks such as "sit," "down," "shake," or "roll over" using positive reinforcement techniques. Break down each trick into small steps and reward your dog for successful attempts.
- ✓ **Tips:** Keep training sessions short and fun to maintain your dog's interest. Use high-value treats as rewards and praise your dog enthusiastically for their efforts. Be patient and consistent in your training approach.

- ✓ **Benefits:** Stimulates your dog's mind, improves obedience and communication, and strengthens the bond between you and your dog through collaborative learning

10. Indoor Fetch with Soft Toys or Balls

- ✓ **Description:** Play a game of fetch indoors using soft toys or lightweight balls to prevent damage to furniture or belongings. Encourage your dog to retrieve the toy and return it to you.
- ✓ **Tips:** Choose an open area free from obstacles. Use a designated fetch toy to prevent confusion. Start with short distances and gradually increase the challenge.
- ✓ **Benefits:** Provides physical exercise, mental stimulation, and reinforces recall skills in a controlled environment.

11. Interactive Puzzle Toys

- ✓ **Description:** Provide your dog with interactive puzzle toys that dispense treats or require them to solve a puzzle to access food rewards. These toys engage your dog's problem-solving skills and keep them entertained.
- ✓ **Tips:** Start with simple puzzle toys and gradually introduce more challenging ones as your dog becomes proficient. Supervise your dog during play to ensure their safety and prevent frustration. Rotate toys regularly to keep your dog mentally stimulated.
- ✓ **Benefits:** Stimulates cognitive abilities, alleviates boredom, and provides a mentally enriching activity for dogs, especially when left alone.

12. Obstacle Course

- ✓ **Description:** Set up an indoor obstacle course using household items such as chairs, boxes, and tunnels. Guide your dog through the course, encouraging them to navigate obstacles, jump over hurdles, and weave between objects.
- ✓ **Tips:** Start with simple obstacles and gradually increase complexity as your dog gains confidence. Use treats or toys to motivate your dog and reward successful completion of each obstacle. Ensure the course is safe and secure to prevent accidents.
- ✓ **Benefits:** Provides physical exercise, mental stimulation, and improves coordination and agility skills in a fun and interactive way.

13. Bubble Chasing

- ✓ **Description:** Blow bubbles and encourage your dog to chase and pop them. This activity can be entertaining and stimulating for dogs, especially those who enjoy chasing moving objects.
- ✓ **Tips:** Use pet-safe bubbles to avoid any potential harm to your dog. Monitor your dog's excitement level to prevent overstimulation. Supervise the activity to ensure your dog doesn't ingest the bubbles.
- ✓ **Benefits:** Provides mental and physical exercise, encourages movement and playfulness, and offers a novel and entertaining activity for dogs.

14. Indoor Agility Training

- ✓ **Description:** Set up a mini agility course indoors using agility equipment such as tunnels, weave poles, and jumps. Guide your dog through the course, encouraging them to navigate each obstacle.
- ✓ **Tips:** Start with simple obstacles and gradually increase difficulty as your dog becomes more proficient. Use treats or toys to motivate your dog and reward successful completion of each obstacle. Ensure the course is safe and secure to prevent accidents.
- ✓ **Benefits:** Improves coordination, balance, and confidence, provides physical and mental stimulation, and strengthens the bond between you and your dog through cooperative training.

15. Musical Chairs

- ✓ **Description:** Arrange chairs in a circle with one fewer chair than the number of participants (including your dog). Play music and encourage participants to walk around the chairs. When the music stops, everyone must find a chair to sit on. The one left standing is out. Continue until one winner remains.
- ✓ **Tips:** Use upbeat music to keep the game exciting. Encourage your dog to participate by walking around the chairs with you. Use treats or toys to reward your dog for their participation.
- ✓ **Benefits:** Encourages movement and physical activity, stimulates your dog's mind, and provides a fun and interactive game for the whole family, including your furry friend.

16. Dance or Freestyle Routines

- ✓ **Description:** Dance or freestyle routines involve choreographing a series of movements and tricks to music, performed by both you and your dog. These routines can include spins, jumps, weaving between your legs, and other fun moves.
- ✓ **Tips:** Start with simple movements and gradually add complexity as you and your dog become more comfortable. Use positive reinforcement techniques such as treats and praise to encourage your dog during training sessions. Practice in a quiet, distraction-free environment to help your dog focus.
- ✓ **Benefits:** Dance routines provide mental stimulation, physical exercise, and strengthen the bond between you and your dog through collaborative learning and teamwork.

17. Setting up a Mini Agility Course with Cushions and Pillows

- ✓ **Description:** Create a mini agility course indoors using cushions, pillows, and other household items. Design challenges such as jumping over cushions, weaving between pillows, and crawling under low obstacles.
- ✓ **Tips:** Ensure the course is safe and secure, with no sharp edges or unstable items. Start with simple obstacles and gradually increase difficulty as your dog gains confidence. Use treats or toys as incentives to complete each challenge.

- ✓ **Benefits:** Mini agility courses improve coordination, balance, and confidence in your dog. They provide mental and physical stimulation and offer a fun and interactive way to bond with your furry friend.

18. Teaching Your Dog to Tidy Up Toys
- ✓ **Description:** Teach your dog to pick up and put away their toys on command. Start by encouraging your dog to hold a toy in their mouth, then guide them to place it in a designated container or basket.
- ✓ **Tips:** Break down the training process into small steps, rewarding your dog for each successful attempt. Use high-value treats and plenty of praise to reinforce the desired behavior. Be patient and consistent in your training approach.
- ✓ **Benefits:** Teaching your dog to tidy up toys promotes mental stimulation and obedience. It encourages responsibility and independence in your dog and helps keep your living space tidy.

19. Practicing Impulse Control Exercises
- ✓ **Description:** Impulse control exercises involve teaching your dog to resist immediate impulses or urges in favor of more desirable behaviors. This can include exercises such as "leave it," "stay," and "wait."
- ✓ **Tips:** Start with simple exercises and gradually increase difficulty as your dog becomes more proficient. Use positive reinforcement techniques to reward your dog for demonstrating self-control. Practice impulse control exercises regularly to reinforce good behavior.
- ✓ **Benefits:** Impulse control exercises improve self-control and obedience in your dog. They help prevent unwanted behaviors such as jumping, begging, and stealing food. Additionally, they strengthen the bond between you and your dog through positive reinforcement and collaborative learning.

OUTDOOR FUN GAMES

These outdoor activities offer a wide range of options to keep your dog active, engaged, and happy while enjoying the great outdoors. Remember to choose activities that suit your dog's age, fitness level, and preferences, and always prioritize safety and supervision during outdoor adventures.

1. Fetch in the Backyard or Park
- ✓ **Description:** Play a game of fetch with your dog using a ball or favorite toy in a backyard or open park area.
- ✓ **Tips:** Choose a safe and enclosed space to prevent your dog from running off. Use a designated fetch toy to avoid confusion.
- ✓ **Precautions:** Watch out for hazards such as uneven terrain or potential obstacles.

- ✓ **Benefits:** Provides physical exercise, mental stimulation, and reinforces recall skills in an outdoor setting.

2. Frisbee Toss and Retrieve

- ✓ **Description:** Toss a Frisbee for your dog to retrieve, promoting running and jumping.
- ✓ **Tips:** Use a soft and dog-friendly Frisbee to prevent injuries. Start with short throws and gradually increase distance.
- ✓ **Precautions:** Avoid playing on hot surfaces to prevent paw burns. Ensure your dog doesn't overexert or jump excessively to prevent injuries.
- ✓ **Benefits:** Enhances agility, coordination, and provides cardiovascular exercise.

3. Agility Training in an Outdoor Space

- ✓ **Description:** Set up agility equipment such as tunnels, hurdles, and weave poles in a spacious outdoor area for training or fun.
- ✓ **Tips:** Start with basic obstacles and gradually increase complexity. Use treats or toys as motivation.
- ✓ **Precautions:** Ensure equipment is sturdy and safe to prevent accidents. Avoid training in extreme weather conditions.
- ✓ **Benefits:** Improves coordination, balance, and confidence while providing physical and mental stimulation.

4. Hiking or Trail Walking

- ✓ **Description:** Explore nature trails or hiking paths with your dog, enjoying outdoor scenery and fresh air.
- ✓ **Tips:** Choose trails suitable for your dog's fitness level and breed. Bring plenty of water and snacks for breaks.
- ✓ **Precautions:** Watch out for wildlife, ticks, and rough terrain. Keep your dog on a leash where required.

- ✓ **Benefits:** Provides physical exercise, mental stimulation, and strengthens the bond between you and your dog through shared experiences.

5. Swimming or Water Play (if your dog enjoys it and it's safe)

- ✓ **Description:** Allow your dog to swim or play in water, such as lakes, rivers, or dog-friendly beaches.
- ✓ **Tips:** Start in shallow water and gradually increase depth. Use a canine life jacket for safety, especially for inexperienced swimmers.
- ✓ **Precautions:** Supervise your dog at all times. Be mindful of currents, tides, and water quality.
- ✓ **Benefits:** Provides low-impact exercise, cools your dog in hot weather, and can be therapeutic for dogs with joint issues.

6. Interactive Water Toys or Sprinklers

- ✓ **Description:** Set up water sprinklers or water toys in your backyard for your dog to chase and play with.
- ✓ **Tips:** Choose toys designed for dogs and ensure they are safe and durable. Supervise your dog to prevent ingestion of water or toys.
- ✓ **Precautions:** Monitor your dog's activity to prevent overexertion or dehydration.
- ✓ **Benefits:** Offers a refreshing way for your dog to cool off in hot weather while providing mental and physical stimulation.

7. Outdoor Scent Work or Tracking Games

- ✓ **Description:** Hide treats or toys in outdoor areas and encourage your dog to find them using their sense of smell.
- ✓ **Tips:** Start with easy hiding spots and gradually increase difficulty. Use high-value rewards to maintain interest.
- ✓ **Precautions:** Avoid areas with potential hazards or toxic substances. Watch out for wildlife or other animals.
- ✓ **Benefits:** Stimulates your dog's sense of smell, provides mental enrichment, and offers a rewarding activity for dogs of all ages.

8. Dog-Friendly Parkour or Urban Agility

- ✓ **Description:** Practice urban agility or parkour by navigating outdoor obstacles such as benches, stairs, and railings.
- ✓ **Tips:** Start with basic obstacles and ensure they are safe and stable. Use positive reinforcement to encourage exploration.
- ✓ **Precautions:** Watch out for traffic, pedestrians, and other hazards in urban environments. Avoid areas with broken or unsafe structures.

- ✓ **Benefits:** Improves confidence, balance, and coordination while providing mental and physical stimulation in real-world environments.

9. Flirt Pole Games in a Spacious Outdoor Area

- ✓ **Description:** Use a flirt pole—a long pole with a toy attached—to engage your dog in chase and play.
- ✓ **Tips:** Choose an open and safe area free from obstacles. Control the intensity of play to prevent overexertion or injury.
- ✓ **Precautions:** Avoid abrupt movements to prevent strain or injury. Use a sturdy flirt pole and supervise closely during play.
- ✓ **Benefits:** Provides high-intensity exercise, mental stimulation, and strengthens the bond between you and your dog through interactive play.

10. Dock Diving or Retrieving Toys from Water

- ✓ **Description:** Train your dog to jump off a dock and retrieve toys from the water.
- ✓ **Tips:** Start with shallow water and gradually increase depth. Use floating toys designed for water retrieval.
- ✓ **Precautions:** Ensure your dog is a confident swimmer and supervise closely during training sessions. Watch out for strong currents or hazards in the water.
- ✓ **Benefits:** Provides excellent cardiovascular exercise, builds confidence in the water, and strengthens the bond between you and your dog through fun water play.

11. Bikejoring or Canicross (if your dog is suitable and properly trained)

- ✓ **Description:** Attach your dog to a harness and run or bike alongside them while they pull.
- ✓ **Tips:** Start with short sessions and gradually increase distance and speed. Use proper equipment and ensure your dog is properly trained.
- ✓ **Precautions:** Monitor your dog's stamina and avoid overheating or overexertion. Choose suitable trails or paths free from traffic.
- ✓ **Benefits:** Provides vigorous exercise for both you and your dog, strengthens muscles, and improves endurance.

12. Flyball Training or Competitions

- ✓ **Description:** Participate in flyball—a relay race where dogs jump hurdles, retrieve a ball, and return over hurdles.
- ✓ **Tips:** Start with basic training exercises to teach your dog each component of the race. Join a flyball team or club for organized competitions.
- ✓ **Precautions:** Ensure your dog is physically fit and properly warmed up before participating. Use proper jumping techniques to prevent injuries.

- ✓ **Benefits:** Enhances agility, speed, and teamwork skills, provides mental stimulation, and fosters camaraderie among team members.

13. Outdoor Obedience or Agility Competitions

- ✓ **Description:** Participate in outdoor obedience or agility competitions where dogs showcase their skills in various exercises or obstacle courses.
- ✓ **Tips:** Prepare your dog through consistent training and practice. Familiarize yourself with competition rules and requirements.
- ✓ **Precautions:** Ensure your dog is physically fit and mentally prepared for the competition environment. Follow safety guidelines provided by event organizers.
- ✓ **Benefits:** Offers an opportunity for dogs and handlers to demonstrate their training achievements, fosters camaraderie among participants, and provides a platform for skill development.

14. Canine Freestyle or Dancing Routines in a Park or Open Space

- ✓ **Description:** Choreograph and perform dance routines with your dog, incorporating music, movement, and synchronized actions.
- ✓ **Tips:** Start with simple moves and gradually add complexity. Use positive reinforcement to encourage desired behaviors.
- ✓ **Precautions:** Avoid excessive strain on your dog's joints or muscles. Provide plenty of water and breaks during practice sessions.
- ✓ **Benefits:** Enhances coordination, strengthens the bond between you and your dog through shared activities, and provides a creative outlet for expression.

15. Group Playdates or Dog Park Outings with Other Friendly Dogs

- ✓ **Description:** Arrange playdates with other dog owners or visit dog parks where your dog can socialize and interact with other friendly dogs.
- ✓ **Tips:** Choose playmates that match your dog's size, temperament, and play style. Supervise interactions to ensure safety and intervene if necessary.
- ✓ **Precautions:** Watch for signs of stress, aggression, or bullying behavior in either your dog or other dogs. Be prepared to remove your dog from any situation that becomes unsafe.
- ✓ **Benefits:** Provides opportunities for socialization, exercise, and mental stimulation, promotes positive behavior around other dogs, and helps prevent loneliness or boredom.

16. Disc Dog Competitions

- ✓ **Description:** Participate in disc dog competitions where dogs and their handlers showcase skills in disc throwing and catching.
- ✓ **Tips:** Practice throwing techniques and train your dog to catch discs reliably. Familiarize yourself with competition rules and scoring criteria.

- ✓ **Precautions:** Ensure discs are safe for your dog to catch and avoid overexertion during training or competition.
- ✓ **Benefits:** Enhances coordination between you and your dog, provides mental and physical exercise, and offers opportunities for teamwork and skill development.

17. Cross-Country Running or Hiking

- ✓ **Description:** Go for long-distance running or hiking sessions with your dog, exploring diverse terrain and landscapes.
- ✓ **Tips:** Start with shorter distances and gradually increase as both you and your dog build stamina. Bring water, snacks, and proper gear for both of you.
- ✓ **Precautions:** Monitor your dog's condition for signs of fatigue or overheating. Be prepared for weather changes and plan routes accordingly.
- ✓ **Benefits:** Provides excellent cardiovascular exercise for both you and your dog, strengthens endurance and stamina, and fosters a deeper bond through shared experiences.

18. Nature Walks or Exploring New Outdoor Environments

- ✓ **Description:** Take leisurely walks in natural settings such as forests, meadows, or nature reserves, allowing your dog to explore new sights and scents.
- ✓ **Tips:** Choose trails suitable for your dog's fitness level and mobility. Bring essentials such as water, waste bags, and insect repellent.
- ✓ **Precautions:** Watch out for wildlife, poisonous plants, or environmental hazards. Keep your dog on a leash where required and respect local regulations.
- ✓ **Benefits:** Provides sensory stimulation, mental enrichment, and opportunities for bonding with your dog in serene outdoor surroundings.

19. Camping or Outdoor Overnight Trips with Your Dog

- ✓ **Description:** Go camping or plan outdoor overnight trips with your dog, enjoying nature together.
- ✓ **Tips:** Choose dog-friendly campsites or outdoor destinations. Pack essentials such as food, water, bedding, and safety gear.
- ✓ **Precautions:** Be aware of wildlife and other potential hazards. Keep your dog on a leash or under control at all times.
- ✓ **Benefits:** Provides opportunities for bonding, adventure, and shared experiences with your dog in natural surroundings.

Chapter 2: Understanding Canine Behavior

2.1 Exploring Canine Psychology

Understanding canine psychology is essential for interpreting and addressing a dog's behavior effectively. Dogs are social animals with intricate social hierarchies, having evolved alongside humans for thousands of years. This evolution has shaped their behavior to communicate and cooperate with us effectively. Dogs rely heavily on their senses, particularly their keen sense of smell, to gather information about their environment and human emotions. Additionally, they are highly attuned to body language and vocal cues, enabling them to interpret and respond to human communication signals. Emotions play a significant role in canine behavior, with dogs experiencing a range of emotions such as joy, fear, anxiety, and contentment. Recognizing and understanding these emotions is crucial for addressing behavioral issues and promoting overall well-being. Furthermore, genetics, early experiences, and environmental factors all influence a dog's behavior. Genetic predispositions may make certain breeds more prone to specific behaviors, while early socialization and training play a critical role in shaping a dog's behavior and developing appropriate social skills.

Key Insights into Canine Psychology

Learning Processes. Dogs learn through a combination of classical conditioning, operant conditioning, and observational learning. Classical conditioning involves associating two stimuli, such as a bell ringing (neutral stimulus) with food (unconditioned stimulus), leading to the bell alone eliciting a conditioned response (salivation). Operant conditioning involves learning through consequences, where behaviors are reinforced (strengthened) or punished (weakened) based on their consequences. Observational learning occurs when dogs observe and mimic the behaviors of other dogs or humans, which can influence their own behavior.

Emotional Responses. Dogs experience a range of emotions similar to humans, including happiness, fear, anger, sadness, and excitement. Emotional responses can influence behavior, as dogs may react differently depending on their emotional state. For example, a fearful dog may exhibit avoidance behaviors or aggression if it feels threatened, while a happy dog may display playful behaviors.

Social Structure and Communication. Dogs are pack animals with a hierarchical social structure. Understanding pack dynamics and communication signals is essential for interpreting and responding appropriately to dog behavior. Canine communication includes vocalizations (such as barking, growling, and whining), body language (including posture, facial expressions, and tail wagging), and scent marking. Dogs use these signals to convey information about their intentions, emotions, and social status.

Problem Behaviors. Certain behaviors, such as aggression, fearfulness, separation anxiety, and destructive chewing, may arise due to underlying psychological or emotional issues. It's essential to address these behaviors with positive reinforcement training, behavior modification techniques, and, if necessary, professional guidance from a certified dog behaviorist or trainer.

Individual Differences. Just like humans, each dog is unique, with its own temperament, personality, and behavioral quirks. While breed tendencies and genetic predispositions may influence behavior to some extent, it's essential to recognize and respect the individuality of each dog. Factors such as early socialization, training methods, and environmental enrichment can all shape a dog's personality and behavior over time.

Cognitive Abilities. Dogs possess cognitive abilities that enable problem-solving, memory retention, and learning from past experiences. Understanding these cognitive processes can enhance training techniques and improve communication between dogs and their owners.

Stress and Coping Mechanisms. Dogs experience stress in various situations, and their ability to cope with stress varies from one individual to another. Recognizing signs of stress and implementing strategies to alleviate it are essential for promoting a dog's well-being and preventing behavioral issues.

Socialization Periods. Puppies undergo critical socialization periods during their early development, where exposure to different environments, people, and animals shapes their social skills and behavior. Providing positive socialization experiences during these periods is vital for raising well-adjusted and sociable dogs.

Territorial Behavior. Dogs exhibit territorial behaviors to establish and defend their territory. Understanding the motivations behind territorial behavior can help owners manage and modify these behaviors appropriately, ensuring harmonious coexistence within the household and community.

Attachment and Bonding. Dogs form strong attachments and bonds with their owners, influencing their behavior and emotional well-being. Nurturing these bonds through positive reinforcement, companionship, and affection fosters a trusting and secure relationship between dogs and their owners.

Sensory Enrichment. Providing sensory enrichment activities, such as puzzle toys, scent games, and novel experiences, stimulates a dog's senses and cognitive abilities, promoting mental stimulation and reducing boredom and destructive behavior.

Communication Styles. Each dog has its unique communication style, including how they express emotions, desires, and needs. Learning to interpret and respond to a dog's communication cues strengthens the bond between owners and their dogs, facilitating effective communication and understanding.

Adaptability and Resilience. Dogs demonstrate remarkable adaptability and resilience in response to changes in their environment or routine. Supporting dogs through transitions and challenges with patience, consistency, and positive reinforcement builds their confidence and resilience over time.

2.2 Recognizing Reactive and Aggressive Behaviors

Recognizing reactive and aggressive behaviors in dogs is crucial for maintaining their well-being and ensuring the safety of both humans and other animals. Reactive behaviors typically stem from fear, anxiety, or frustration, while aggressive behaviors involve threats or actual harm towards a person, animal, or object. One common reactive behavior is excessive barking or growling when a dog feels threatened or overwhelmed. This behavior serves as a warning signal, indicating that the dog is uncomfortable with the situation and may escalate to aggression if not addressed appropriately. Other reactive behaviors include pacing, panting, trembling, or attempts to escape the situation.

Aggressive behaviors can manifest in various forms, including lunging, snapping, biting, or displaying dominant postures such as standing tall with ears erect and tail raised. Aggression may be directed towards strangers, family members, other animals, or even specific objects or situations. Understanding the triggers and underlying motivations behind aggression is essential for developing effective management and intervention strategies, which may include implementing behavior modification techniques, providing appropriate socialization and training, creating safe environments to reduce triggers, and utilizing desensitization and counterconditioning methods. Recognizing signs of distress or discomfort in dogs is key to identifying potential reactive or aggressive behaviors. These signs may include dilated pupils, flattened ears, raised fur along the back, lip licking, yawning, or avoidance behaviors such as turning away or trying to hide.

Early intervention and proactive management are crucial for addressing reactive and aggressive behaviors in dogs. This may involve implementing behavior modification techniques, providing appropriate socialization and training, and seeking guidance from a qualified professional, such as a certified dog behaviorist or trainer.

2.3 Exploring Different Types of Canine Aggression

Throughout this chapter, we identify different types of canine aggression, delineating actionable steps for each specific behavior. These measures aim to address the root causes of aggression while fostering a safe and supportive environment for both the dog and its human companions. Additionally, we emphasize the importance of seeking guidance from qualified professionals, such as veterinarians or certified animal behaviorists, to ensure the implementation of effective strategies tailored to the individual dog's needs and circumstances. By integrating expert consultations with hands-on interventions, dog owners can navigate the complexities of canine aggression with confidence and compassion, paving the way for a happier and healthier bond between humans and their canine companions.

1. Territorial Aggression. Dogs may exhibit territorial aggression in response to perceived threats to their territory, such as strangers approaching their home or possessions. This behavior is often characterized by defensive postures, vocalizations, and warning signals to deter intruders.

> **Actions to take:** Create a safe space for the dog, limit access to territorial spaces, provide desensitization training to strangers, use calming commands, and redirect the dog's behavior in potential threat situations.

2. Fear Aggression. Fear aggression occurs when a dog reacts aggressively to perceived threats or situations that induce fear or anxiety. Dogs may display defensive behaviors such as growling, lunging, or biting in an attempt to remove themselves from the perceived threat or defend against it.

> **Actions to take:** Use desensitization and counterconditioning techniques to reduce fear associated with feared situations, avoid stressful situations when possible, provide a safe and predictable environment, use calming commands, and distraction to redirect the dog's behavior.

3. Resource Guarding. Resource guarding involves aggressive behaviors aimed at protecting valuable resources such as food, toys, or resting areas. Dogs may growl, snarl, or even bite when someone approaches or attempts to take away their prized possessions.

> **Actions to take:** Avoid provoking the dog when near resources, use positive reinforcement to teach the dog to willingly surrender resources, exchange valuable items with better rewards, maintain a stable and predictable feeding routine.

4. Dog-Directed Aggression. Some dogs exhibit aggression towards other dogs, either due to fear, past negative experiences, or socialization deficits. Dog-directed aggression may occur during encounters with unfamiliar dogs, while on-leash walks, or in multi-dog households.

> **Actions to take:** Avoid conflict situations with other dogs, use positive reinforcement to teach the dog to behave appropriately during encounters with other dogs, provide opportunities for controlled and positive social interactions.

5. Redirected Aggression. Redirected aggression occurs when a dog redirects its aggressive behavior towards a person or animal that was not the original target of its frustration or arousal. This may happen when a dog is unable to access the source of its frustration, such as during barrier frustration or when prevented from engaging in a desired behavior.

> **Actions to take:** Avoid physically intervening during a dog's state of agitation, reduce environmental stimulation that could cause frustration, provide the dog with an appropriate outlet for its energy through play or physical exercise.

6. Predatory Aggression. Predatory aggression is motivated by a dog's natural hunting instinct and may manifest as chasing, stalking, or attacking small animals, wildlife, or even small children or objects perceived as prey. This behavior can be dangerous and requires careful management and training to prevent harm to others.

> **Actions to take:** Supervise the dog closely when outdoors, use a leash or long line for control, provide mental and physical stimulation to reduce predatory drive, redirect the dog's focus with toys or games, and reinforce appropriate behavior.

7. Pain-Induced Aggression. Dogs experiencing pain or discomfort may exhibit aggression as a defensive response to being touched or approached. It's essential to rule out any medical conditions or injuries that may be causing pain and address them promptly to prevent further aggression.

> **Actions to take:** Immediately seek veterinary care to address underlying medical issues causing pain, avoid handling the dog in painful areas, provide a comfortable and quiet resting area, administer prescribed medications as directed by the veterinarian.

8. Maternal Aggression. Maternal aggression occurs in female dogs protecting their puppies from perceived threats. This behavior is instinctual and serves to ensure the survival of offspring. While maternal aggression is natural, it's essential to provide a safe and stress-free environment for the mother and her puppies.

> **Actions to take:** Limit interactions with unfamiliar individuals near the mother and her puppies, provide a secure and quiet whelping area, avoid handling the puppies excessively, monitor the mother's stress levels, and provide support and guidance to the mother as needed.

9. Inter-Male Aggression. Male dogs may display aggression towards other males, particularly during territorial disputes, competition for resources, or mating-related encounters. This behavior is often influenced by social hierarchies and reproductive instincts.

> **Actions to take:** Manage the environment to reduce triggers for aggression, provide outlets for physical and mental stimulation, use positive reinforcement to reward calm and non-aggressive behavior, avoid confrontational situations with other males.

10. Sexual Aggression. Some dogs may exhibit sexual aggression, which manifests during mating periods or in the presence of dogs in heat. This type of aggression can lead to aggressive behaviors towards other dogs or even towards people in certain situations.

> **Actions to take:** Neuter the dog to reduce hormonal-driven aggression, provide appropriate outlets for sexual frustration through exercise and mental stimulation, avoid situations that may trigger aggressive behavior, and seek guidance from a veterinarian or behaviorist.

11. Fear-Induced Reactivity. Although often associated with fear, fear-induced reactivity may differ from outright aggression. However, dogs reactive to fear can display aggressive behaviors when they feel threatened or unable to escape from a frightening situation.

> **Actions to take:** Gradually expose the dog to feared stimuli using desensitization and counterconditioning techniques, provide a safe retreat area, avoid punishment for fearful behavior, use positive reinforcement to reward calm and relaxed behavior.

12. Medical Aggression. Some dogs may become aggressive due to medical conditions or injuries causing pain or discomfort. This type of aggression is often a defensive response to the vulnerability caused by illness or pain.

> **Actions to take:** Seek immediate veterinary care to address underlying medical conditions causing pain or discomfort, follow prescribed treatment plans, and provide a calm and supportive environment for the dog's recovery.

13. Idiopathic Aggression. In some cases, dogs may exhibit aggressive behaviors without an apparent cause or clear motivation. This type of aggression, also known as idiopathic aggression, can be challenging to diagnose and manage, requiring thorough evaluation by experienced animal behavior professionals.

> **Actions to take:** Conduct a thorough behavioral assessment by a qualified professional, implement a behavior modification plan tailored to the dog's needs, provide environmental enrichment, and ensure the dog's physical and mental well-being are prioritized.

2.4 Considering the Role of Breed in Behavior

Understanding the role of breed in canine behavior is crucial for dog owners and professionals alike as it sheds light on the intricate relationship between breed and behavior, debunking myths and providing insights into the nuanced nature of canine temperament and personality. Each dog breed is associated with specific traits and characteristics that have been selectively bred for over generations. For example, herding breeds like Border Collies exhibit a strong instinct to control the movement of other animals, while retrievers such as Labrador Retrievers are known for their friendly and outgoing nature. These breed-specific traits can offer valuable insights into a dog's behavior tendencies, yet they should not be viewed as deterministic of individual temperament. While genetics play a role in shaping a dog's behavior, it's important to understand that genetic predispositions do not dictate a dog's entire personality. Genetic factors may influence traits such as prey drive, aggression levels, and sociability, but environmental factors and individual experiences also play significant roles in shaping behavior. Therefore, while certain breeds may have a higher likelihood of exhibiting specific behaviors, individual variation within breeds is substantial. The environment in which a dog is raised plays a pivotal role in shaping its behavior. Factors such as socialization, training methods, living conditions, and owner interactions all contribute to a dog's temperament and personality. A well-socialized dog from a breed known for aggression may exhibit friendly and non-aggressive behavior, while a poorly socialized dog from a typically docile breed may display fearfulness or aggression. One common misconception is the notion that a dog's breed alone determines its behavior and temperament. This oversimplified view has led to unfair stereotypes and discrimination against certain breeds, such as Pit Bulls and Rottweilers, which are often unjustly labeled as inherently aggressive. In reality, individual dogs within these breeds can vary widely in temperament, and breed-specific legislation based on stereotypes is ineffective and unjust. It's essential to recognize that each dog is an individual with its own unique personality, regardless of breed. While breed characteristics may provide a general overview of what to expect, it's crucial to assess each dog based on its individual temperament, experiences, and behavior. Factors such as socialization, training, and environmental enrichment play significant roles in shaping a dog's behavior and should be considered alongside breed tendencies.

Understanding the role of breed in canine behavior requires a nuanced approach that acknowledges the interplay between genetics, environment, and individual variation. While breed-specific traits can offer insights into a dog's predispositions, they do not determine its entire personality.

2.5 Interpreting Your Dog's Body Language

Interpreting your dog's body language is a fundamental skill for understanding your canine companion's emotions and intentions. Dogs communicate primarily through nonverbal cues, including body posture, facial expressions, tail wagging, and vocalizations. By learning to interpret these signals accurately, you can better understand your dog's state of mind and respond appropriately to their needs.

1. Body Posture. A dog's body posture can convey a wealth of information about their emotional state. A relaxed and loose posture indicates comfort and contentment, while a tense or stiff posture may indicate fear, aggression, or discomfort. Pay attention to your dog's body language during different situations to gauge their level of comfort and confidence.

2. Facial Expressions. Dogs use facial expressions to communicate a range of emotions, from joy and excitement to fear and anxiety. A relaxed mouth, soft eyes, and relaxed facial muscles indicate a calm and contented dog. Conversely, a wrinkled forehead, raised lips, or bared teeth may signal stress, fear, or aggression. Take note of subtle changes in your dog's facial expressions to understand how they are feeling in various situations.

3. Tail Wagging. Contrary to popular belief, a wagging tail does not always indicate happiness. The position, speed, and direction of your dog's tail wag can convey different meanings. A slow, low wag may indicate insecurity or apprehension, while a fast, high wag may signal excitement or arousal. The position and movement of a dog's tail can provide further clues about its emotional state. For instance, a high, stiffly wagging tail might indicate dominance or excitement, while a low or tucked tail could suggest fear or submission. Additionally, observing whether the tail is erect, lowered, or even tucked can add further insights into its emotional response to certain situations. Pay attention to the context in which your dog is wagging their tail to accurately interpret their emotional state.

4. Vocalizations. While dogs primarily rely on body language to communicate, vocalizations such as barking, growling, and whining can also provide valuable insights into their emotions. Barking can indicate excitement, alarm, or territorial behavior, while growling may signal discomfort, fear, or aggression. Whining or whimpering may indicate pain, anxiety, or a desire for attention. Pay attention to the pitch, intensity, and duration of your dog's vocalizations to understand their underlying emotions.

5. Ear Position. A dog's ears can provide insights into their emotional state. Erect ears may indicate attentiveness or interest, while lowered ears can indicate submission, fear, or anxiety. Also, observe whether the ears are forward-facing or backward-facing, as this can provide further clues about the dog's emotional state.

6. Body Movement. In addition to overall posture, also observe the dog's body movement. For example, a slow and relaxed approach may indicate curiosity or a desire for interaction, while rapid and jerky movements could indicate fear or nervousness.

7. Mouth. Take note if your dog excessively drools or pants, as this could be a sign of discomfort, nausea, or stress. Furthermore, the way the dog holds its mouth can provide additional clues about its emotional state, such as a slight hint of a smile when relaxed or clenched jaws when tense or stressed.

8. Eye Contact. Eye contact can also be an important form of body language for dogs. Some dogs may avoid eye contact when feeling threatened or insecure, while others may actively seek eye contact as a sign of trust and connection.

9. Context and Consistency. It's essential to consider the context in which your dog is exhibiting certain body language cues and to look for patterns of behavior over time. For example, if your dog consistently displays fearful body language in specific situations, such as during visits to the veterinarian or encounters with unfamiliar dogs, it may indicate a fear or anxiety-related issue that requires attention. By observing your dog's body language in various contexts and situations, you can gain a deeper understanding of their emotions and behavior patterns.

10. Building a Strong Bond. Interpreting your dog's body language not only helps you understand their needs and emotions but also strengthens the bond between you and your canine companion. By paying attention to subtle cues and responding empathetically to your dog's signals, you can build trust and communication, fostering a deeper connection and mutual understanding.

2.6 Nurturing Well-Rounded Puppies through Positive Socialization

Ensuring a well-rounded upbringing for puppies involves more than just providing basic care and training. Positive socialization plays a pivotal role in shaping a puppy's behavior, temperament, and overall well-being. In this section, we delve into the importance of socialization and provide guidance on how to create positive socialization experiences for puppies.

- ✓ **Early Socialization.** Early socialization is critical for puppies, as it sets the foundation for their future behavior and interactions with the world around them. During the sensitive developmental period between 3 to 14 weeks of age, puppies are particularly receptive to new experiences and can quickly adapt to various stimuli. Exposing puppies to a wide range of people, animals, environments, sounds, and objects during this time helps them become confident, well-adjusted adults.

- ✓ **Positive Experiences.** Socialization should focus on creating positive associations with new experiences. Expose puppies to different environments, such as parks, streets, and indoor spaces, gradually and with positive reinforcement. Encourage interactions with friendly and well-behaved dogs of various sizes, breeds, and ages to promote positive social skills and prevent fear or aggression towards other dogs.

- ✓ **Gentle Handling.** It's essential to accustom puppies to being handled gently and positively from an early age. This includes handling their paws, ears, mouth, and body to prepare them for grooming, veterinary visits, and other necessary care routines. Make these experiences enjoyable by pairing handling with treats, praise, and play to build trust and confidence in puppies.

- ✓ **Puppy Classes.** Enrolling puppies in puppy socialization classes can provide structured opportunities for socialization and learning. These classes offer supervised play sessions with other puppies, as well as guidance from experienced trainers on basic obedience, manners, and problem-solving skills. Additionally, interacting with different handlers and learning in a group setting helps puppies develop valuable social skills and impulse control.

- ✓ **Exposure to Novel Stimuli.** Introduce puppies to novel stimuli in a controlled and positive manner to build resilience and confidence. Expose them to various surfaces, sounds, textures, and objects, ensuring that each experience is rewarding and non-threatening. Gradually increase the complexity and intensity of stimuli as puppies grow older to continue challenging and enriching their socialization experiences.

- ✓ **Supervision and Safety.** While socializing puppies, prioritize their safety and well-being at all times. Monitor interactions with unfamiliar dogs and environments closely, intervening if necessary to prevent negative experiences or conflicts. Ensure that puppies have positive encounters with people of all ages and backgrounds, teaching them to be comfortable and well-mannered in diverse social settings.

- ✓ **Exposure to Various Environments.** Introduce your puppy to a wide range of environments, including different indoor and outdoor settings, urban and rural areas, as well as various surfaces such as grass, pavement, gravel, and sand. This exposure helps them become comfortable and adaptable in different surroundings.

- ✓ **Interaction with Different People.** Encourage positive interactions with people of diverse ages, genders, ethnicities, and appearances. This helps puppies develop confidence and friendliness towards unfamiliar individuals, reducing the likelihood of fear or aggression towards strangers.

- ✓ **Socialization with Other Animals.** Arrange supervised encounters with other dogs and animals, ensuring that these interactions are positive and safe. This exposure teaches puppies appropriate social behavior and helps prevent fear or aggression towards other animals in adulthood.

- ✓ **Exposure to Different Sounds.** Introduce your puppy to various sounds, including household noises, traffic, construction, fireworks, and thunderstorms. Gradually expose them to these sounds at a low volume and increase intensity over time to prevent fear or anxiety associated with loud noises.

- ✓ **Positive Reinforcement Training.** Use positive reinforcement techniques, such as treats, praise, and toys, to reinforce desired behaviors during socialization experiences. This creates positive associations with new experiences and encourages puppies to approach unfamiliar situations with confidence.

- ✓ **Handling and Grooming.** Regularly handle and groom your puppy, including activities such as brushing, nail trimming, and ear cleaning. This helps them become comfortable with being touched and handled, making veterinary visits and grooming sessions less stressful in the future.

- ✓ **Structured Socialization Classes.** Enroll your puppy in structured socialization classes or puppy kindergarten programs led by experienced trainers. These classes provide opportunities for supervised socialization with other puppies and guidance from professionals on proper behavior and training techniques.

- ✓ **Monitoring Stress Levels.** Pay close attention to your puppy's body language and behavior during socialization experiences. If you notice signs of stress or anxiety, such as trembling, panting, lip licking, or avoidance behaviors, provide reassurance and remove them from the stressful situation if necessary.

- ✓ **Consistency and Patience.** Socialization is an ongoing process that requires consistency, patience, and positive reinforcement. Be patient with puppies as they navigate new experiences and environments, providing support and guidance as needed. Celebrate their successes and progress, no matter how small, to reinforce positive behavior and encourage continued learning and growth.

- ✓ **Individualized Approach.** Recognize that each puppy is unique and may have different socialization needs based on factors such as breed, personality, and past experiences. Tailor socialization experiences to suit the individual needs and comfort level of each puppy, gradually exposing them to new stimuli at their own pace. Avoid overwhelming puppies with too many new experiences or overly stressful situations, as this can hinder rather than enhance socialization.

By prioritizing positive socialization experiences during puppyhood, owners can lay the foundation for a well-adjusted, confident, and socially adept adult dog. Investing time and effort in socialization pays off in the long run, fostering strong bonds and enriching the lives of both puppies and their human companions.

Chapter 3: Training Principles and Techniques

3.1 The Fundamentals of Dog Training

Dog training is a captivating journey, a harmonious dance between human and canine, where communication, patience, and understanding play vital roles. At its core lies positive reinforcement, a powerful tool that rewards desired behaviors, encouraging their repetition. Whether it's a tasty treat, a playful game, or a warm word of praise, positive reinforcement creates a delightful link between action and consequence in a dog's mind. Consistency is the cornerstone of successful training. Dogs thrive on routine and predictability, so it's crucial to establish clear rules and expectations. From the timing of rewards to the cues used to signal desired behaviors, consistency provides a solid framework for learning. It's akin to teaching a dance routine – the steps must remain the same for the performance to flow smoothly. However, training demands more than just consistency; it requires patience – lots of it. Dogs don't become experts overnight; they need time to learn and grow. Like tending to a delicate plant, training necessitates gentle care, understanding that progress may come in small, incremental steps. Setbacks are part of the journey, not obstacles, but opportunities for reflection and adjustment. Communication serves as the bridge that connects trainer and dog. Clear, concise cues or commands, accompanied by appropriate body language and tone, facilitate understanding. It's akin to having a conversation without words – relying on gestures, expressions, and tone to convey meaning.

A well-timed cue or a gentle touch can speak volumes to a dog, fostering trust and cooperation. Understanding motivation is crucial for unlocking a dog's potential. Just as each person has unique preferences and desires, so too does each dog. Some may leap for joy at the sight of a tasty treat, while others may prefer a game of tug-of-war or a belly rub. Discovering what motivates a dog fuels the training process, ensuring engagement and enthusiasm every step of the way. Training is a journey of gradual progression, starting with simple tasks and building upon them over time. Like ascending a staircase, each successful repetition brings the dog closer to mastery. Breaking down complex behaviors into smaller, manageable steps prevents overwhelm and builds confidence. It's a voyage of discovery and growth, brimming with moments of triumph and joy. However, beyond the mechanics of training lies a deeper purpose – building a bond. Training sessions are not merely about teaching commands; they're opportunities for bonding and relationship building. Positive interactions, trust, and mutual respect lay the foundation of a robust bond, enriching both human and canine lives. In essence, dog training is an art form, a symphony of communication, patience, and connection.

3.2 Different Types of Dog Training

Each type of dog training has its own principles, techniques, and applications, and the most effective approach may vary depending on the dog's temperament, behavior, and training goals. By exploring and understanding the different types of dog training, owners can select the methods that best suit their dog's needs and preferences. Our tips and instructions aim to provide guidance on how to effectively implement each type of dog training while fostering a positive and rewarding experience for both you and your canine companion.

1. Positive Reinforcement Training. Positive reinforcement training focuses on rewarding desired behaviors to encourage their repetition. This approach utilizes rewards such as treats, praise, toys, or playtime to reinforce behaviors that owners want to see more of. By associating positive consequences with desired actions, dogs learn to willingly perform the desired behaviors.

Tips:

- ✓ Use high-value treats or rewards that your dog finds particularly enticing.
- ✓ Timing is crucial; reward the desired behavior immediately to reinforce it effectively.
- ✓ Be consistent in rewarding the behavior you want to encourage.
- ✓ Incorporate verbal praise and enthusiastic body language to enhance the positive association.

2. Clicker Training. Clicker training is a form of positive reinforcement training that uses a small handheld device called a clicker to mark desired behaviors with a distinct sound. The clicker serves as a precise and consistent marker to indicate to the dog that they have performed the correct behavior, followed by a reward. Clicker training is especially effective for shaping behaviors and teaching complex tricks.

Tips:
- ✓ Start by associating the clicker sound with treats by clicking and then immediately offering a treat.
- ✓ Click at the precise moment your dog performs the desired behavior to mark it.
- ✓ Follow the click with a reward to reinforce the behavior.
- ✓ Gradually phase out the need for treats by intermittently rewarding with praise or other rewards.

3. Marker Training. Marker training, similar to clicker training, uses a verbal marker such as the word "yes" or a clicker to signal desired behaviors. The marker serves as a bridge between the desired behavior and the reward, helping to communicate to the dog precisely what behavior is being rewarded.

Tips:
- ✓ Choose a clear and distinct marker word or sound, such as "yes" or a clicker.
- ✓ Use the marker consistently to signal to your dog that they have performed the correct behavior.
- ✓ Follow the marker with a reward to reinforce the behavior.
- ✓ Practice with various behaviors to ensure your dog understands the meaning of the marker.

4. Negative Reinforcement Training. Negative reinforcement training involves removing or avoiding aversive stimuli to increase the likelihood of desired behaviors. This approach relies on the principle that dogs will repeat behaviors that lead to the cessation or avoidance of discomfort or unpleasantness. While negative reinforcement can be effective when used correctly, it requires careful application to avoid causing stress or fear in dogs.

Tips:
- ✓ Identify a discomfort or aversive stimulus that your dog wants to avoid, such as a leash tug.
- ✓ Apply the stimulus until your dog performs the desired behavior, then immediately remove it.
- ✓ Pair the removal of the aversive stimulus with a reward to reinforce the desired behavior.
- ✓ Use negative reinforcement sparingly and ensure it does not cause distress or fear in your dog.

5. Punishment-Based Training. Punishment-based training involves applying aversive consequences to discourage unwanted behaviors. Methods such as leash corrections, verbal reprimands, or physical corrections are used to deter dogs from engaging in behaviors deemed undesirable. However, punishment-based training can lead to stress, anxiety, and aggression in dogs if applied incorrectly or excessively.

Tips:

- ✓ Clearly communicate to your dog which behaviors are undesirable.
- ✓ Apply punishment consistently and immediately after the undesired behavior occurs.
- ✓ Use punishment techniques that are safe and humane, avoiding physical or verbal abuse.
- ✓ Focus on rewarding alternative, desirable behaviors rather than solely punishing unwanted behaviors.

6. Relationship-Based Training. Relationship-based training focuses on building a strong bond and mutual trust between the dog and the owner. This approach emphasizes positive interactions, clear communication, and understanding the dog's needs and preferences. Relationship-based training prioritizes cooperation and collaboration between the dog and the owner, fostering a harmonious relationship built on trust and respect.

Tips:

- ✓ Focus on building trust and cooperation with your dog through positive interactions.
- ✓ Spend quality time bonding with your dog through activities such as play, walks, and training sessions.
- ✓ Use clear communication and avoid using fear or intimidation as motivators.
- ✓ Respect your dog's individual preferences and needs, fostering a strong and mutually respectful relationship.

7. Marker Word Training. Marker word training involves using a specific verbal cue or marker word, such as "good" or "yes," to signal to the dog that they have performed the desired behavior. Similar to clicker training, marker word training provides clear and consistent feedback to the dog, helping to reinforce the correct behaviors.

Tips:

- ✓ Select a marker word that is distinct and easily recognizable to your dog.
- ✓ Consistently use the marker word to signal to your dog when they have performed the desired behavior.
- ✓ Immediately follow the marker word with a reward to reinforce the behavior.
- ✓ Practice with various behaviors to ensure your dog understands the meaning of the marker word.

8. Science-Based Training. Science-based training methods are grounded in principles of animal behavior and learning theory. These methods prioritize positive reinforcement and reward-based techniques supported by empirical evidence and research. Science-based training emphasizes understanding the underlying motivations and behaviors of dogs to inform training practices effectively.

Tips:

- ✓ Familiarize yourself with principles of animal behavior and learning theory to inform your training practices.
- ✓ Prioritize positive reinforcement and reward-based techniques supported by empirical evidence.
- ✓ Use systematic and structured training approaches based on scientific research.
- ✓ Continuously evaluate and adjust your training methods based on your dog's responses and behavior.

9. Balance Training. Balance training combines elements of both positive reinforcement and correction-based techniques to achieve training goals. This approach seeks to strike a balance between rewarding desired behaviors and correcting unwanted behaviors when necessary. Balance training aims to provide clear communication and guidance to the dog while maintaining a respectful and cooperative relationship.

Tips:

- ✓ Combine elements of positive reinforcement and correction-based techniques in a balanced manner.
- ✓ Focus on reinforcing desired behaviors while providing clear guidance and correction for unwanted behaviors.
- ✓ Ensure that corrections are fair, consistent, and do not cause distress or fear in your dog.
- ✓ Strive to maintain a positive and cooperative relationship with your dog throughout the training process.

10. Motivational Training. Motivational training focuses on identifying and utilizing the specific motivations and drives of individual dogs to facilitate learning and behavior modification. By understanding what motivates a dog, such as food, toys, or social interaction, trainers can effectively leverage these incentives to encourage desired behaviors.

Tips:

- ✓ Identify your dog's specific motivations, such as food, toys, or social interaction.
- ✓ Use these motivators to reinforce desired behaviors during training sessions.
- ✓ Experiment with different rewards to determine what most effectively motivates your dog.
- ✓ Keep training sessions fun and engaging to maintain your dog's enthusiasm and focus.

11. Bond-Based Training. Bond-based training emphasizes building a strong emotional bond and connection between the dog and the owner as the foundation for training. This approach prioritizes positive interactions, mutual trust, and understanding to strengthen the relationship and facilitate effective communication and cooperation during training sessions.

Tips:

- ✓ Prioritize building a strong emotional bond and connection with your dog.

- ✓ Spend quality time together engaging in activities that strengthen your relationship.
- ✓ Use positive reinforcement and clear communication to build trust and cooperation.
- ✓ Approach training as an opportunity to deepen your bond and understanding of each other.

12. Behavior Adjustment Training (BAT). Behavior Adjustment Training (BAT) focuses on modifying reactive or fearful behavior by allowing the dog to make choices and learn to cope with triggers at a safe distance. This approach empowers the dog to control its environment and responses, ultimately leading to more confident and relaxed behavior.

Tips:
- ✓ Use desensitization and counterconditioning techniques to change the dog's emotional response to triggers gradually. This involves exposing the dog to the trigger at a distance where they remain calm and relaxed, then gradually decreasing the distance as they become more comfortable.
- ✓ Allow the dog to approach or retreat from triggers based on their comfort level, rewarding calm and relaxed behavior. This helps the dog build positive associations with previously feared stimuli and learn that they have control over their environment
- ✓ Be patient and consistent in your approach, gradually increasing the difficulty of the exercises as the dog progresses. Remember that every dog learns at its own pace, so tailor the training to suit your dog's individual needs and abilities.

13. Canine Fitness Training. Canine fitness training focuses on improving a dog's physical health, strength, and flexibility through exercises and activities tailored to their needs. This type of training not only enhances the dog's physical well-being but also promotes mental stimulation and improves their overall quality of life.

Tips:
- ✓ Incorporate a variety of exercises, such as balance work, strength training, and flexibility exercises, to improve overall fitness. This includes activities like balance discs, wobble boards, cavaletti poles, and stretches.
- ✓ Use positive reinforcement to encourage participation and make the training sessions enjoyable for your dog. Offer treats, praise, or play as rewards for completing exercises or showing effort. This will motivate your dog to participate actively and eagerly in their fitness routine.
- ✓ Start slowly and gradually increase the intensity and duration of exercises as your dog builds strength and stamina. Pay attention to your dog's physical condition and adjust the training regimen accordingly to prevent injury and ensure their safety.

14. Service Dog Training. Service dog training involves teaching specific tasks to assist individuals with disabilities or special needs. These tasks can range from guiding the visually impaired to alerting to seizures or providing mobility assistance. Service dogs undergo rigorous training to perform their duties reliably and safely in various environments.

Tips:

- ✓ Break down complex tasks into smaller, manageable steps, using positive reinforcement to teach each component. Start with foundational skills such as obedience commands and gradually introduce task-specific training.

- ✓ Provide extensive socialization and exposure to various environments and stimuli to ensure the dog can perform reliably in different situations. This includes exposure to crowded places, loud noises, other animals, and various surfaces.

- ✓ Use a variety of training methods and techniques, including shaping, capturing, and targeting, to teach specific tasks effectively. Tailor the training approach to suit the individual dog's temperament, abilities, and learning style.

- ✓ Maintain consistency and patience throughout the training process, celebrating each success and providing support and encouragement during setbacks. Building a strong bond and mutual trust with the dog is essential for successful service dog training.

15. Agility Training. Agility training involves navigating obstacle courses with speed and precision, requiring coordination, focus, and teamwork between the dog and handler. This dynamic and fast-paced sport not only provides physical exercise but also mental stimulation and strengthens the bond between dog and owner.

Tips:

- ✓ Start with basic agility equipment, such as jumps and tunnels, gradually increasing the complexity of the course as the dog gains confidence and skill. Introduce new obstacles one at a time, ensuring the dog understands how to navigate each element before moving on to the next.

- ✓ Use toys, treats, or other rewards to motivate and reward the dog for successfully completing obstacles. Positive reinforcement encourages the dog to engage enthusiastically in the training process and builds confidence in tackling new challenges.

- ✓ Focus on building clear communication and trust between you and your dog, as agility is a team sport that relies on mutual understanding and cooperation. Practice obedience commands and directional cues to guide your dog through the course smoothly and efficiently.

- ✓ Keep training sessions fun and varied to maintain your dog's enthusiasm and focus. Incorporate games, breaks, and plenty of praise to make agility training an enjoyable experience for both you and your dog.

3.3 Tailoring Training Approaches to Your Dog's Breed and Personality

Understanding that every dog is unique, with its own set of traits, tendencies, and personality quirks, is essential when it comes to training. While there are universal principles and techniques that apply to all dogs, tailoring your approach to match your dog's breed and individual personality can significantly enhance the effectiveness and success of training sessions. Different dog breeds have been selectively bred for specific purposes over generations, resulting in distinct characteristics and behaviors. For example, herding breeds like Border Collies may exhibit high energy levels and a strong instinct to chase, stemming from their history of herding livestock. On the other hand, retrievers such as Labradors or Golden Retrievers may display a natural inclination to retrieve objects, owing to their lineage as hunting companions. Understanding these breed-specific traits can provide valuable insights into your dog's behavior and help you anticipate their responses during training sessions. Moreover, breed characteristics can influence your training approach. For instance, while herding breeds thrive on mental and physical stimulation, they may become easily bored or frustrated if their needs for exercise and mental challenges are not met. Therefore, training sessions with such breeds should incorporate activities that engage their minds and bodies, such as agility exercises or interactive games that simulate their natural instincts. Conversely, breeds bred for companionship or as family pets, like Cavalier King Charles Spaniels or Bichon Frises, may exhibit a strong desire to please their owners and enjoy social interactions. Training methods for these breeds may focus more on positive reinforcement and building a strong bond with their owners, as they are often motivated by praise, affection, and rewards. Just as humans have unique personalities, so do dogs. Some may be outgoing and confident, while others are more reserved and sensitive. Understanding your dog's individual personality traits can provide valuable insights into their behavior and preferences, allowing you to tailor your training methods to suit their needs effectively.

Observing your dog's behavior and temperament is key to understanding their personality. Pay attention to how they react to various stimuli, such as new environments, unfamiliar people, or other animals. A dog that eagerly explores new surroundings and eagerly interacts with strangers may have an outgoing and sociable personality, while one that hesitates or withdraws may be more reserved or cautious. Moreover, identifying your dog's motivators is essential for successful training. Some dogs may be highly food-motivated, eagerly performing tasks in exchange for treats, while others may be more toy-driven or motivated by praise and attention. By understanding what motivates your dog, you can tailor your training approach to leverage their preferences effectively. For example, a food-motivated dog may respond well to treat-based training methods, where desirable behaviors are rewarded with tasty treats or food rewards. On the other hand, a dog that is motivated by play and toys may be more engaged in training sessions that incorporate interactive toys or games as rewards for desired behaviors.

In conclusion, tailoring your training approach to match your dog's breed and individual personality is essential for effective and successful training outcomes. By understanding your dog's breed-specific traits and personality characteristics, you can adapt your training methods to suit their unique needs and preferences, ultimately strengthening the bond between you and your canine companion.

3.4 Avoiding Common Training Mistakes

Training your dog can be a rewarding experience, but it's essential to be aware of common pitfalls that can hinder progress and cause frustration for both you and your canine companion:

- ✓ **Inconsistency.** Consistency is key in dog training. Inconsistencies in your commands, rules, or rewards can confuse your dog and undermine the effectiveness of your training efforts. It's crucial to establish clear expectations and remain consistent in your approach throughout the training process.

- ✓ **Lack of Patience.** Training takes time and patience. Rushing through exercises or expecting instant results can lead to frustration for both you and your dog. Remember that learning is a gradual process, and each dog learns at their own pace. Be patient and persistent, and celebrate small victories along the way.

- ✓ **Overwhelming Your Dog.** Introducing too many commands or training exercises at once can overwhelm your dog and hinder their progress. Focus on one skill or behavior at a time, gradually increasing the difficulty as your dog masters each task. Keep training sessions short and engaging to maintain your dog's focus and enthusiasm.

- ✓ **Using Punishment Incorrectly.** Punishment-based training techniques, such as yelling or physical corrections, can be detrimental to your dog's well-being and may lead to fear or aggression. Instead of focusing on punishment, emphasize positive reinforcement to encourage desired behaviors. Rewarding good behavior is more effective and promotes a positive learning experience for your dog.

- ✓ **Neglecting Socialization.** Proper socialization is crucial for a well-rounded and well-behaved dog. Exposing your dog to different people, animals, environments, and experiences helps prevent fear and anxiety-related behaviors. Make socialization a priority from an early age and continue to expose your dog to new situations throughout their life.

- ✓ **Ignoring Health and Exercise Needs.** A healthy dog is more receptive to training. Ensure your dog receives regular exercise, mental stimulation, and proper nutrition to support their physical and mental well-being. Neglecting these needs can lead to boredom, frustration, and unwanted behaviors.

- ✓ **Skipping Training Sessions.** Consistent training is essential for maintaining good behavior and reinforcing learned skills. Skipping training sessions or becoming complacent can result in regression or the development of bad habits. Make training a regular part of your routine and commit to regular practice sessions with your dog.

- ✓ **Failing to Adapt to Your Dog's Needs.** Every dog is unique, with different personalities, learning styles, and motivations. It's essential to tailor your training approach to suit your dog's individual needs and preferences. Be flexible and willing to adjust your methods as needed to ensure a positive and productive training experience for both you and your dog.

- ✓ **Neglecting Mental Stimulation.** Dogs not only need physical exercise but also mental stimulation to stay mentally sharp and engaged. Neglecting mental stimulation can lead to boredom and the development of destructive behaviors. Incorporate activities that challenge your dog's mind, such as puzzle toys, scent games, or training sessions that require problem-solving. Engaging your dog's brain can help prevent behavioral issues and strengthen the bond between you and your furry friend.

By avoiding these common training mistakes and adopting a patient, consistent, and positive approach, you can set yourself and your dog up for success in training. Remember that building a strong bond and mutual trust is at the core of effective training, so prioritize communication, understanding, and respect in your interactions with your canine companion.

Chapter 4: Tailored Training Programs

4.1 Designing Training Programs for Pets of All Ages

When it comes to designing training programs for pets of all ages, it's essential to consider the unique developmental stages and individual needs of each animal. Whether you're working with a playful puppy, an energetic adolescent, or a mature adult dog, tailoring your approach to their age-specific requirements is crucial for successful training outcomes.

Puppyhood. Puppies are like sponges, soaking up information from their environment and experiences. During this critical period, focus on socialization, basic obedience, and building positive associations with people, animals, and various stimuli. Short, frequent training sessions that incorporate play and rewards are ideal for keeping puppies engaged and motivated.

Adolescence. Adolescence is a challenging stage characterized by increased independence and boundary-pushing behavior. While adolescents may test limits and exhibit more stubbornness, it's essential to remain patient and consistent in your training efforts. Reinforce previously learned behaviors while introducing more advanced commands and impulse control exercises to help channel their energy constructively.

Adulthood. Adult dogs typically have a better attention span and impulse control than puppies or adolescents. Training during this stage can focus on refining obedience skills, addressing any behavior issues that may have emerged, and introducing more complex tasks or activities. Tailor the training program to match the dog's personality, preferences, and lifestyle to ensure continued engagement and success.

4.2 Addressing Specific Training Needs for Older Dogs

Training older dogs presents unique challenges and opportunities due to factors such as physical limitations, established behaviors, and changing cognitive abilities. Understanding and addressing these specific training needs are crucial for promoting mental stimulation, physical well-being, and overall quality of life in senior canine companions.

1. Assessing Physical Health. Before embarking on a training program for older dogs, it's essential to assess their physical health and any age-related conditions they may have. Consult with a veterinarian to identify any mobility issues, joint pain, or sensory impairments that may impact training activities. Design training exercises that accommodate their physical limitations while promoting gentle exercise and mobility.

2. Adapting to Cognitive Changes. Aging can affect a dog's cognitive function, leading to changes in memory, learning ability, and attention span. Be patient and understanding when training older dogs, allowing them extra time to process information and respond to cues. Break training sessions into shorter, more manageable segments to prevent mental fatigue and frustration.

3. Focusing on Mental Stimulation. Incorporate training activities that provide mental stimulation and enrichment for older dogs. Puzzle toys, scent games, and interactive training exercises can help keep their minds sharp and engaged. Rotate training activities regularly to prevent boredom and stimulate their cognitive function.

4. Addressing Age-Related Behaviors. Older dogs may exhibit age-related behaviors such as increased vocalization, house soiling, or changes in sleep patterns. Address these behaviors with patience and understanding, using positive reinforcement techniques to encourage desired behaviors. Consult with a professional trainer or behaviorist for guidance on managing and modifying age-related behaviors effectively.

5. Maintaining Physical Fitness. While older dogs may have reduced energy levels and mobility, it's essential to maintain their physical fitness through appropriate exercise and activity. Design training programs that focus on low-impact exercises such as gentle walks, swimming, or stretching to help keep their muscles strong and joints flexible. Avoid high-impact activities that may exacerbate joint pain or cause injury.

6. Emphasizing Positive Reinforcement. Positive reinforcement remains the cornerstone of effective training for older dogs. Use praise, treats, and rewards to reinforce desired behaviors and encourage learning. Focus on building a trusting and cooperative relationship with your senior dog, emphasizing encouragement and support throughout the training process.

7. Adjusting Training Goals. Recognize that older dogs may have different training goals and priorities compared to younger counterparts. Instead of focusing solely on obedience or performance tasks, consider training exercises that promote mental stimulation, social interaction, and bonding with their owners. Adjust training goals and expectations to align with the individual needs and capabilities of your senior dog.

8. Monitoring Health and Progress. Regularly monitor your older dog's health and progress during training sessions. Be vigilant for signs of discomfort, fatigue, or stress, and adjust training activities accordingly. Communicate regularly with your veterinarian and trainer to ensure that your senior dog's training program remains safe, effective, and tailored to their evolving needs.

9. Pain Management. If your senior dog suffers from joint pain or other painful conditions, ensure to adapt training to reduce movements that may cause discomfort. Use soft cushions or mats during exercises and provide frequent rest periods during training sessions.

10. Respect Rest Times. Seniors may need more rest and sleep during the day. Schedule training sessions at times when your dog is most alert and responsive, avoiding overloading them with too many activities.

11. Adapt Home Environment. Modify the home environment to make training your senior dog easier. Remove any obstacles or hazards that could cause falls or accidents and ensure that accessories and equipment used during training are safe and comfortable for your dog.

12. Maintain Routines. Seniors often benefit from stable and predictable routines. Try to keep training session times consistent and provide a consistent structure throughout the day, helping your dog feel secure and comfortable.

13. Consider Nutritional Needs. Proper nutrition is crucial for the health and well-being of senior dogs. Ensure that your dog receives a balanced diet tailored to their nutritional needs, as this can directly impact their energy and ability to actively participate in training sessions.

4.3 Implementing Effective Training Strategies for Rescue Dogs

Rehabilitating rescue dogs through positive reinforcement techniques is a compassionate and effective approach to helping them overcome past traumas and develop into well-adjusted companions. Unlike punitive methods, positive reinforcement focuses on rewarding desired behaviors, building trust, and fostering a positive relationship between the dog and their caregiver. One of the primary goals of rehabilitating rescue dogs is to rebuild their confidence and trust in humans. Positive reinforcement techniques, such as using treats, praise, and toys to reward good behavior, help create positive associations with interactions and training sessions. By consistently rewarding desired behaviors, rescue dogs learn to trust and feel safe in their new environment. Rescued dogs often exhibit hyper-vigilance, aggression towards other dogs, or noise sensitivity as a result of their past experiences. Hyper-vigilance, characterized by constant scanning of the environment and heightened reactivity to stimuli, can be managed through gradual exposure to new environments and stimuli paired with positive reinforcement. For example, if a rescued dog is hypersensitive to loud noises, such as thunderstorms or fireworks, desensitization techniques can be employed by gradually exposing the dog to recorded sounds at a low volume while providing treats and praise to create positive associations. Aggression towards other dogs may stem from fear, insecurity, or lack of socialization. Counterconditioning techniques can help address this behavior by pairing the presence of other dogs with positive experiences, such as treats or play, to change the dog's emotional response. For instance, if a rescued dog displays aggression towards other dogs on walks, the owner can use counterconditioning by rewarding calm behavior in the presence of other dogs and gradually decreasing the distance between them over time. Noise sensitivity, common in rescued dogs due to past traumatic experiences, can be managed through desensitization and counterconditioning. Gradual exposure to noises paired with positive reinforcement can help the dog develop a more positive association with the sounds. For example, if a rescued dog is sensitive to sudden noises, the owner can gradually introduce the noise at a low volume while providing treats and praise to create positive associations and reduce anxiety. Patience and consistency are paramount when rehabilitating rescue dogs. These dogs may have experienced neglect, abuse, or abandonment, leading to fear, anxiety, and uncertainty. As such, progress may be slow, and setbacks are to be expected. It's essential to approach training with empathy and understanding, allowing the dog to progress at their own pace.

Tailoring training methods to suit the individual needs and personalities of rescue dogs is crucial for success. Each dog will have their own triggers, fears, and areas for improvement. By observing the dog's behavior and responses, caregivers can adjust training techniques accordingly, ensuring they are effective and well-received. Incorporating enrichment activities into the rehabilitation process is also beneficial for rescue dogs. Activities such as puzzle games, scent work, and interactive toys provide mental stimulation, alleviate boredom, and help build confidence. These activities engage the dog's mind and encourage them to explore their environment in a positive and rewarding way. Consistent socialization is essential for rehabilitating rescue dogs. Exposure to new people, animals, and environments in a controlled and positive manner helps desensitize dogs to unfamiliar stimuli and builds their confidence in various situations. Gradually introducing them to new experiences while providing support and reassurance helps them feel more comfortable and secure. Above all, rehabilitating rescue dogs requires a compassionate and understanding approach. By focusing on positive reinforcement, patience, and empathy, caregivers can help these dogs heal from past traumas and thrive in their new homes. Each small step forward is a testament to the resilience of rescue dogs and the power of positive training methods.

Implementing Effective Training Strategies for Rescue Dogs

Implementing Effective Training Strategies for Rescue Dogs requires special attention and sensitivity due to their unique backgrounds and experiences. These dogs may come from various environments, including shelters, abusive situations, or neglectful homes, which can impact their behavior and trust in humans. Implementing effective training strategies for rescue dogs involves patience, understanding, and a tailored approach to address their specific needs.

1. Build Trust and Confidence. Prioritize building trust and confidence with your rescue dog before diving into formal training. Spend time bonding with your dog through gentle interactions, offering treats, and providing a safe and nurturing environment. Building a strong foundation of trust is essential for successful training outcomes.

2. Establish a Routine. Establishing a consistent routine can help rescue dogs feel secure and reduce anxiety. Set a schedule for feeding, exercise, training sessions, and rest, providing structure and predictability in their daily lives. Consistency in routine can also facilitate learning and behavioral progress.

3. Start with Basic Commands. Begin training with basic obedience commands such as "sit," "stay," and "come." These commands provide a foundation for communication and establish boundaries for your rescue dog. Use positive reinforcement techniques such as treats, praise, and toys to encourage desired behaviors and gradually increase the complexity of commands as your dog progresses.

4. Focus on Desensitization and Counterconditioning. Many rescue dogs may have fears or anxieties related to past experiences. Use desensitization and counterconditioning techniques to help them overcome these fears gradually. Expose your dog to triggers in a controlled and positive manner, pairing the experience with rewards to create positive associations and reduce fear responses.

5. Patience and Consistency. As we said before, training rescue dogs requires patience and consistency. Understand that progress may be slow, and setbacks are normal. Celebrate small victories and remain consistent in your training approach, reinforcing positive behaviors while gently correcting unwanted ones. Avoid becoming frustrated or discouraged, as this can undermine your dog's confidence and progress.

6. Seek Professional Guidance. Consider seeking guidance from a professional dog trainer or behaviorist experienced in working with rescue dogs. They can provide valuable insights, personalized training plans, and support tailored to your dog's specific needs and challenges. A professional trainer can also offer guidance on managing any behavioral issues that may arise during training.

7. Promoting Socialization. Socialization is crucial for rescue dogs to help them feel comfortable and confident in various environments and with different people and animals. Gradually expose your dog to new experiences, people, and animals in a controlled and positive manner, ensuring their safety and well-being throughout the process.

8. Understanding Trauma and Behavior. Explore in more detail how past trauma can influence the behavior of rescued dogs. Discuss the effects of trauma on attachment, self-confidence, and reactions to stressful events.

9. Tailoring Training to Individual Needs. Emphasize the importance of tailoring training to the individual needs of each rescued dog. Each dog will have a unique background and may require a customized approach to address their specific challenges.

10. Managing Fear and Anxiety. Dedicate a section to managing fear and anxiety in rescued dogs. Provide tips on how to recognize signs of stress and anxiety in dogs and how to use relaxation and comfort techniques to help them overcome these negative emotions.

11. Gradual Exposure Therapy. Delve deeper into the concept of gradual exposure therapy and illustrate how it can be effectively used in rescued dog training. Explain how to plan and conduct gradual exposure sessions to help dogs overcome their fears safely and gradually.

12. Building Confidence Through Success. Discuss the importance of building rescued dogs' confidence through success. Show how to encourage dogs to make small progress and how to celebrate every success, no matter how small, to reinforce their self-confidence and belief in the training process.

4.4 Case Studies

Case Study 1: Overcoming Fear Aggression in a Rescued Dog

Background: Max, a 4-year-old mixed breed dog, was rescued from an abusive home where he experienced physical and emotional trauma. Upon arrival at the shelter, Max displayed fear aggression towards humans and other dogs, making him difficult to handle and adopt out.

Training Approach:

✓ **Building Trust and Confidence:** The training team focused on building trust and confidence with Max through positive reinforcement techniques. They spent time sitting quietly with him, offering treats and gentle praise to create positive associations with human interaction.

✓ **Establishing a Routine:** A consistent routine was established for Max, providing him with structure and predictability. Regular feeding times, exercise sessions, and training activities helped reduce his anxiety and improve his overall behavior.

✓ **Starting with Basic Commands:** Max was taught basic obedience commands such as "sit" and "stay" using positive reinforcement methods. Treats and praise were used to reward desired behaviors, gradually increasing his confidence and responsiveness.

✓ **Focusing on Desensitization and Counterconditioning:** Max's fear aggression towards other dogs was addressed through desensitization and counterconditioning techniques. Under the guidance of a professional trainer, Max was exposed to other dogs at a safe distance while receiving treats and praise for calm behavior.

✓ **Patience and Consistency:** The training team exhibited patience and consistency in working with Max, understanding that progress would take time. They celebrated small victories and remained committed to his rehabilitation journey, even during setbacks.

Results: After several weeks of dedicated training and rehabilitation efforts, Max showed significant improvement in his behavior. He became more relaxed and comfortable around humans and other dogs, demonstrating reduced fear aggression and increased socialization skills. Max was successfully adopted by a loving family who continued his training and provided him with a supportive and nurturing home environment. Today, Max enjoys a happy and fulfilling life, thanks to the effective training techniques and compassionate care he received during his rehabilitation journey.

Case Study 2: Addressing Noise Sensitivity in a Rescued Dog

Background: Luna, a 2-year-old Labrador Retriever mix, was rescued from a hoarding situation where she was exposed to loud noises and chaotic environments. As a result, Luna developed severe noise sensitivity, exhibiting signs of distress and anxiety during thunderstorms or fireworks.

Training Approach:

✓ **Desensitization Training:** The training team implemented a desensitization training program to help Luna overcome her fear of loud noises. They started by playing recorded sounds of thunderstorms at a low volume while engaging Luna in enjoyable activities, such as playing with her favorite toys or receiving treats.

✓ **Gradual Exposure:** Over time, the volume of the recorded sounds was gradually increased, always ensuring that Luna remained relaxed and comfortable. The goal was to desensitize Luna to the sounds of thunderstorms by associating them with positive experiences and rewards.

✓ **Counterconditioning:** In addition to desensitization, counterconditioning techniques were used to change Luna's emotional response to loud noises. Whenever Luna heard the sound of thunderstorms or fireworks, she was immediately rewarded with treats and praise to create positive associations.

Results: After several weeks of consistent desensitization and counterconditioning training, Luna showed significant improvement in her response to loud noises. She became less anxious and more relaxed during thunderstorms, demonstrating a reduced fear response. Luna's adoptive family continued her training at home, providing her with a safe and supportive environment during loud noise events. With ongoing reinforcement of her training techniques, Luna continued to make progress and live a happier, more confident life.

Case Study 3: Managing Separation Anxiety in a Rescued Dog

Background: Bailey, a 3-year-old Terrier mix, was surrendered to a shelter due to severe separation anxiety. Whenever left alone, Bailey would exhibit destructive behavior, such as chewing furniture and excessive barking, resulting in distress for both Bailey and his owners.

Training Approach:

✓ **Gradual Departure Training:** The training team implemented a gradual departure training program to help Bailey become more comfortable with being alone. They started by leaving Bailey alone for short periods, gradually increasing the duration over time.

✓ **Providing Enrichment:** To keep Bailey mentally stimulated during periods of alone time, the training team provided him with interactive toys, puzzle feeders, and chew toys. These activities helped redirect Bailey's focus and alleviate boredom.

✓ **Using Calming Techniques:** Calming techniques, such as playing soothing music or leaving an item with the owner's scent, were used to help Bailey relax during periods of separation. These techniques helped create a calming environment and reduce Bailey's anxiety.

Results: Through consistent training and implementation of calming techniques, Bailey showed significant improvement in his separation anxiety. He became more comfortable being alone and exhibited reduced destructive behavior. Bailey's owners continued to reinforce his training techniques and provide him with a supportive environment at home. With ongoing practice and patience, Bailey's separation anxiety continued to diminish, allowing him to enjoy a more peaceful and stress-free life.

4.5 Providing Recommended Reading, Websites, and Training Tools

Access to reliable and informative resources is essential for dog owners seeking to deepen their knowledge and refine their training skills. Here, we compile a comprehensive list of recommended reading materials, reputable websites, and innovative training tools to support owners on their journey towards fostering a harmonious relationship with their canine companions.

1. Recommended Reading

- **"The Other End of the Leash: Why We Do What We Do Around Dogs" by Patricia B. McConnell:** This insightful book explores the intricate dynamics of human-canine communication and offers practical guidance for understanding and responding to your dog's behavior.

- **"Culture Clash" by Jean Donaldson:** Renowned dog trainer Jean Donaldson delves into the complexities of canine behavior and provides evidence-based strategies for addressing common training challenges.

- **"Inside of a Dog: What Dogs See, Smell, and Know" by Alexandra Horowitz:** Delve into the fascinating world of canine cognition and perception with this illuminating book, offering fresh insights into how dogs experience the world around them.

- **"Don't Shoot the Dog!: The New Art of Teaching and Training" by Karen Pryor:** Renowned animal trainer Karen Pryor introduces readers to the principles of positive reinforcement training and its transformative impact on behavior modification.

- **"How to Behave So Your Dog Behaves" by Dr. Sophia Yin:** Dr. Sophia Yin's comprehensive guide offers practical advice for fostering cooperative and harmonious relationships with dogs through effective communication and positive reinforcement.
- **"Decoding Your Dog: Explaining Common Dog Behaviors and How to Prevent or Change Unwanted Ones" by American College of Veterinary Behaviorists:** This collaborative work by leading veterinary behaviorists provides valuable insights into canine behavior, addressing common issues and offering evidence-based solutions for pet owners.
- **"The Power of Positive Dog Training" by Pat Miller:** Pat Miller advocates for positive reinforcement-based training methods, highlighting the effectiveness of reward-based approaches in fostering cooperative and harmonious relationships between dogs and their owners.
- **"The Dog Listener: Learning the Language of Your Best Friend" by Jan Fennell:** Jan Fennell introduces readers to the concept of "Amichien Bonding," emphasizing the importance of understanding and respecting the natural instincts and communication signals of dogs to establish trust and cooperation.
- **"Click to Calm: Healing the Aggressive Dog" by Emma Parsons:** Emma Parsons offers a compassionate and effective approach to managing and modifying aggressive behavior in dogs using clicker training and positive reinforcement techniques.
- **"Before and After Getting Your Puppy: The Positive Approach to Raising a Happy, Healthy, and Well-Behaved Dog" by Dr. Ian Dunbar:** Dr. Ian Dunbar provides practical guidance for every stage of puppyhood, from preparation and socialization to basic training and problem-solving, using positive, science-based methods to nurture well-rounded and confident dogs.

2. **Reputable Websites**
   - **The Association of Professional Dog Trainers (APDT):** Access a wealth of resources, articles, and educational materials on dog training and behavior from certified professionals.
   - **The American Kennel Club (AKC):** Explore breed-specific information, training resources, and expert advice on obedience, agility, and other dog sports.
   - **Karen Pryor Clicker Training:** Learn about the science of clicker training and discover innovative techniques for teaching new behaviors and strengthening the human-animal bond.
   - **Victoria Stilwell Positively:** Renowned dog trainer Victoria Stilwell shares positive reinforcement training tips, behavior advice, and success stories to inspire and empower dog owners.
   - **The Whole Dog Journal:** Stay informed with evidence-based articles, product reviews, and training tips from experienced canine professionals dedicated to promoting holistic dog care.

- **Dog Star Daily:** Dog Star Daily features a variety of training resources, including articles, videos, and podcasts, covering topics ranging from puppy training to behavior modification for adult dogs.
- **Fear Free Pets:** Fear Free Pets offers educational resources and training programs designed to reduce fear, anxiety, and stress in pets, promoting a positive and fear-free veterinary experience.
- **Dr. Sophia Yin's Website:** Dr. Sophia Yin's website offers a wealth of training tips, behavior guides, and resources for pet owners, along with access to her groundbreaking
- **Low Stress Handling certification program for veterinary professionals. The International Association of Animal Behavior Consultants (IAABC):** The IAABC website provides information on certified animal behavior consultants, along with articles, webinars, and resources for addressing behavior issues in companion animals.
- **The Pet Professional Guild:** The Pet Professional Guild advocates for force-free, science-based training methods and offers educational resources, training courses, and networking opportunities for pet professionals and enthusiasts.

3. Innovative Training Tools

- **Clicker Training:** Utilize a clicker device paired with positive reinforcement to mark desired behaviors and facilitate effective communication during training sessions.
- **Treat Dispensing Toys:** Engage your dog's natural foraging instincts and provide mental stimulation with interactive treat dispensing toys designed to encourage problem-solving and physical activity.
- **Interactive Training Apps:** Access a variety of interactive training apps offering guided exercises, behavior tracking tools, and instructional videos to support ongoing training efforts.
- **Target Sticks and Mats:** Incorporate target sticks and mats into training routines to teach precise behaviors, shaping techniques, and boundary control with clear visual cues.
- **Puzzle Games and Enrichment Toys:** Stimulate your dog's mind and prevent boredom with a diverse range of puzzle games and enrichment toys designed to challenge their cognitive abilities and promote problem-solving skills.
- **Agility Equipment:** Set up agility equipment such as tunnels, jumps, weave poles, and A-frames to create a dynamic and stimulating training environment for your dog. Agility training not only builds physical strength and coordination but also enhances focus, confidence, and teamwork between you and your dog.
- **Balance Boards:** Balance boards are excellent tools for improving proprioception, core strength, and stability in dogs. By teaching your dog to balance on a wobbly surface, you can help them develop better body awareness and control, which can be beneficial for performance sports and injury prevention.

- **Scent Detection Kits:** Engage your dog's sense of smell and natural hunting instincts with scent detection kits or scent work training materials. These kits typically include a variety of scent samples and training aids to help teach your dog to search for and indicate the presence of specific scents, making it an enjoyable and mentally stimulating activity for them.

- **Remote Training Collars:** Remote training collars, also known as e-collars or electronic collars, provide a way to deliver consistent and timely corrections or cues to your dog from a distance. When used correctly and responsibly, remote training collars can be effective tools for reinforcing commands, managing behavior, and improving off-leash control during training sessions.

- **Fitness and Exercise Equipment:** Invest in fitness and exercise equipment tailored to your dog's needs and abilities, such as balance balls, wobble boards, or canine treadmills. These tools can help improve your dog's physical fitness, strength, and flexibility, making them better equipped to participate in various activities and sports while reducing the risk of injury.

Chapter 5: Health and Wellness

In this chapter, we delve into the critical aspects of maintaining optimal health and wellness for your canine companion. From nutrition to emergency care, we explore the various facets that contribute to your dog's overall well-being. Prioritizing your dog's health is essential for ensuring a long, happy, and fulfilling life together. Let's begin by examining the importance of nutrition for optimal health.

5.1 Prioritizing Nutrition for Optimal Health

Nutrition plays a fundamental role in supporting your dog's overall health and well-being. Providing a balanced and nutritious diet is key to promoting longevity, vitality, and disease prevention in dogs. In this chapter, we will explore the essential components of a healthy canine diet and how to ensure your dog receives the nutrients they need to thrive. Dogs require a balanced diet that provides essential nutrients such as protein, carbohydrates, fats, vitamins, and minerals. The specific nutritional needs of your dog may vary based on factors such as age, breed, size, and activity level. Consulting with your veterinarian can help you determine the optimal diet for your dog's unique needs. Selecting high-quality commercial dog foods or preparing homemade meals using wholesome ingredients is crucial for meeting your dog's nutritional needs. Look for dog foods that list meat or meat meals as the primary ingredients and avoid products containing fillers, artificial additives, or excessive amounts of preservatives.

Offering a diverse range of foods ensures that your dog receives a wide array of nutrients essential for their health. Rotate between different protein sources, grains, fruits, and vegetables to provide balanced nutrition and prevent dietary deficiencies. However, be cautious when introducing new foods to avoid gastrointestinal upset. Maintaining an appropriate portion size is vital for preventing obesity and related health issues in dogs. Follow feeding guidelines provided by the food manufacturer or consult with your veterinarian to determine the correct portion size based on your dog's age, weight, and activity level. Avoid overfeeding and monitor your dog's body condition regularly. Access to clean, fresh water is essential for your dog's health and hydration. Ensure that your dog has constant access to water throughout the day, especially during hot weather or after physical activity. Regularly clean and refill your dog's water bowl to prevent contamination and ensure freshness. Pay close attention to your dog's overall health and well-being, as changes in appetite, weight, coat condition, and energy levels can indicate underlying nutritional deficiencies or health issues. Schedule regular veterinary check-ups to monitor your dog's health and address any concerns promptly. In addition to these guidelines, it's essential to prioritize the nutritional needs of dogs with specific health conditions or dietary restrictions. For example, dogs with food allergies or sensitivities may require specialized diets formulated to avoid triggering ingredients. Working closely with your veterinarian or a veterinary nutritionist can help tailor a diet plan that meets your dog's individual needs while addressing any health concerns. Furthermore, consider incorporating supplemental nutrients or dietary additives to support your dog's overall health. Omega-3 fatty acids, glucosamine, and probiotics are examples of supplements that may benefit certain dogs, such as those with joint issues or gastrointestinal sensitivities. However, always consult with your veterinarian before introducing any new supplements to your dog's diet to ensure safety and efficacy.

5.2 Identifying Safe and Unsafe Foods for Dogs

While dogs can enjoy a wide variety of foods, there are some human foods that can be harmful or even toxic to them. In this section, we will explore in detail the safe and unsafe foods for dogs to ensure they receive a diet that supports their overall health.

Safe Foods for Dogs

- ✓ **Lean Proteins:** Lean meats such as chicken, turkey, and beef are excellent sources of protein for dogs. They provide essential amino acids necessary for muscle growth and repair. Cooked eggs are also safe and nutritious for dogs, offering protein, vitamins, and minerals.

- ✓ **Vegetables:** Many vegetables are safe for dogs and provide valuable nutrients such as vitamins, minerals, and fiber. Some examples include carrots, green beans, peas, and sweet potatoes. These vegetables can be served cooked or raw, but it's essential to avoid adding seasonings or oils.

- ✓ **Fruits:** Certain fruits are safe for dogs and can serve as healthy treats. Apples (without seeds), bananas, blueberries, and watermelon are excellent choices. Fruits offer vitamins, antioxidants, and natural sweetness that dogs enjoy.

- ✓ **Whole Grains:** Whole grains like rice, oats, and quinoa are safe for dogs and provide carbohydrates for energy. These grains are also rich in fiber, promoting digestive health. When feeding grains to dogs, ensure they are cooked and free from added sugars or seasonings.
- ✓ **Rice and Potatoes:** Rice and potatoes are easily digestible carbohydrate sources that can be included in the dog's diet to provide energy. Ensure that rice is cooked without any added seasonings, and potatoes are cooked and peeled.
- ✓ **Fish:** Cooked fish such as salmon, tuna, and whitefish can be a healthy addition to a dog's diet. Fish is rich in omega-3 fatty acids, which support heart health, joint function, and skin and coat condition. However, be cautious of fish bones and ensure the fish is thoroughly cooked to avoid the risk of bacterial contamination.
- ✓ **Peanut Butter:** Plain, unsalted peanut butter can be a tasty and nutritious treat for dogs. It's a good source of protein, healthy fats, and vitamins B and E. Peanut butter can be spread on toys or used as a filling for dog-safe treats, but be mindful of added sugars or xylitol, which can be harmful to dogs.
- ✓ **Yogurt:** Plain, unsweetened yogurt can be beneficial for dogs due to its probiotics, which support digestive health. Yogurt is also a good source of calcium and protein. However, be cautious of flavored yogurts, as they may contain added sugars or artificial sweeteners that are not suitable for dogs.
- ✓ **Oatmeal:** Cooked oatmeal is a nutritious and easily digestible option for dogs. It can provide fiber, vitamins, and minerals while also being gentle on the digestive system. Plain, unflavored oatmeal is preferable, as flavored varieties may contain additives or sweeteners that are not suitable for dogs.

Unsafe Foods for Dogs

- ✓ **Chocolate:** Chocolate contains theobromine and caffeine, which are toxic to dogs. Even small amounts of chocolate can cause vomiting, diarrhea, rapid breathing, increased heart rate, seizures, and even death. Dark chocolate and baking chocolate are particularly dangerous.
- ✓ **Grapes and Raisins:** Grapes and raisins can cause kidney failure in dogs, leading to vomiting, diarrhea, lethargy, and loss of appetite. It's essential to avoid feeding grapes or raisins to dogs in any form, including in baked goods or trail mixes.
- ✓ **Onions and Garlic:** Onions and garlic contain compounds that can damage red blood cells in dogs, leading to anemia. Symptoms of onion or garlic toxicity include weakness, vomiting, diarrhea, and pale gums. These ingredients are often found in seasonings, sauces, and soups, so it's crucial to check ingredient labels carefully.
- ✓ **Xylitol:** Xylitol is a sugar substitute found in many sugar-free gums, candies, and baked goods. In dogs, xylitol can cause a rapid release of insulin, leading to hypoglycemia (low blood sugar) and liver failure. Even small amounts of xylitol can be life-threatening for dogs.

- ✓ **Alcohol:** Alcoholic beverages and foods containing alcohol should never be given to dogs. Alcohol ingestion can cause intoxication, vomiting, diarrhea, coordination problems, breathing difficulties, coma, and even death. Keep alcoholic beverages and foods containing alcohol out of reach of pets at all times.
- ✓ **Avocado:** Avocado contains a substance called persin, which can be toxic to dogs in large amounts. While the flesh of ripe avocado is generally considered safe for dogs in small quantities, the pit, skin, and leaves contain higher concentrations of persin and should be avoided.
- ✓ **Coffee and caffeine**: Can cause vomiting, diarrhea, tremors, and in severe cases, heart failure and death.

In addition to these examples, it's essential to be cautious when introducing new foods to your dog's diet. Some seemingly harmless foods may cause gastrointestinal upset or allergic reactions in certain dogs. When in doubt, it's best to consult with your veterinarian before offering new foods to your dog.

5.3 Nutritious Recipes for Homemade Dog Meals

Notes:
- ➢ Please serve these recipes in appropriate portions according to your dog's size and dietary needs.
- ➢ Nutritional values are approximate and may vary based on specific ingredients and serving sizes.

1. Chicken and Sweet Potato Stew

(Setup Time: 15 mins | Cooked in: 25 mins)

This hearty stew combines lean chicken meat with nutrient-rich sweet potatoes, making it a delicious and wholesome meal for dogs. Chicken provides high-quality protein, while sweet potatoes are rich in fiber, vitamins, and minerals, promoting digestive health and providing sustained energy.

Recipe Components:

- ✓ 1 lb boneless, skinless chicken breast, diced
- ✓ 2 medium sweet potatoes, peeled and diced
- ✓ 2 carrots, chopped
- ✓ 1 cup green beans, trimmed and chopped
- ✓ 4 cups low-sodium chicken broth
- ✓ 1 tablespoon olive oil

Preparation Steps: In a large pot, heat olive oil over medium heat. Add diced chicken and cook until browned. Add sweet potatoes, carrots, green beans, and chicken broth to the pot. Bring to a boil, then reduce heat and simmer for 20-25 minutes until vegetables are tender. Allow the stew to cool before serving to your dog. Store any leftovers in an airtight container in the refrigerator for up to 3 days.

Nutritional Info: Protein: 22g, Fat: 5g, Carbohydrates: 18g, Fiber: 3g, Calories: 190 per serving (1 cup)

2. Beef and Barley Casserole

(Setup Time: 20 mins | Cooked in: 50 mins)

This comforting casserole features lean beef and wholesome barley, providing dogs with essential nutrients for muscle health and sustained energy. Beef is a great source of protein and iron, while barley offers fiber and complex carbohydrates to support digestion and overall well-being.

Recipe Components:

- ✓ 1 lb lean ground beef
- ✓ 1 cup barley
- ✓ 2 carrots, peeled and sliced
- ✓ 1 cup frozen peas
- ✓ 4 cups low-sodium beef broth
- ✓ 1 tablespoon olive oil

Preparation Steps: Preheat oven to 350°F (175°C). Grease a casserole dish with olive oil.

In a skillet, brown ground beef over medium heat until cooked through. Drain excess fat. In a large bowl, combine cooked beef, barley, carrots, peas, and beef broth. Pour mixture into the prepared casserole dish. Cover the dish with aluminum foil and bake for 45-50 minutes until barley is tender. Allow the casserole to cool before serving. Refrigerate any leftovers in an airtight container for up to 3 days.

Nutritional Info: Protein: 24g, Fat: 7g, Carbs: 30g, Fiber: 6g, Calories: 260 per serving (1 cup)

3. Turkey and Rice Pilaf

(Setup Time: 15 mins | Cooked in: 25 mins)

This light and flavorful pilaf feature lean turkey meat and brown rice, offering dogs a balanced combination of protein, carbohydrates, and essential nutrients. Turkey is a lean protein source, while brown rice provides fiber and energy to support your dog's active lifestyle.

Recipe Components:
- ✓ 1 lb ground turkey
- ✓ 1 cup brown rice
- ✓ 1 zucchini, diced
- ✓ 1 red bell pepper, diced
- ✓ 4 cups low-sodium chicken broth
- ✓ 1 tablespoon coconut oil

Preparation Steps: In a large skillet, heat coconut oil over medium heat. Add ground turkey and cook until browned. Add brown rice, zucchini, red bell pepper, and chicken broth to the skillet. Bring to a boil, then reduce heat and simmer for 20-25 minutes until rice is cooked through. Allow the pilaf to cool before serving. Store any leftovers in the refrigerator for up to 3 days.

Nutritional Info: Protein: 20g, Fat: 6g, Carb: 24g, Fiber: 3g, Calories: 210 per serving (1 cup)

4. Salmon and Quinoa Salad

(Setup Time: 15 mins | Cooked in: 20 mins for quinoa)

This refreshing salad combines nutrient-rich salmon with protein-packed quinoa, providing dogs with essential omega-3 fatty acids and amino acids. Salmon supports skin and coat health, while quinoa offers a complete source of plant-based protein and fiber for optimal digestion.

Recipe Components:
- ✓ 1 lb cooked salmon, flaked
- ✓ 1 cup cooked quinoa
- ✓ 1 cucumber, diced
- ✓ 1 cup cherry tomatoes, halved

- ✓ 2 tablespoons chopped fresh parsley
- ✓ 1 tablespoon lemon juice

Preparation Steps: In a large bowl, combine cooked salmon, quinoa, cucumber, cherry tomatoes, and parsley. Drizzle lemon juice over the salad and toss gently to combine. Serve the salmon and quinoa salad immediately or refrigerate

Nutritional Info: Calories: 350, Protein: 30g, Carbohydrates: 25g, Fat: 15g, Fiber: 5g

5. Lamb and Vegetable Stir-Fry

(Setup Time: 20 mins | Cooked in: 15 mins)

This stir-fry recipe is packed with lean protein from lamb and an array of colorful vegetables, offering essential vitamins, minerals, and antioxidants. The dish is quick and easy to prepare, making it perfect for a nutritious meal option for your canine companion.

Recipe Components:
- ✓ 1 pound lamb, thinly sliced
- ✓ 2 tablespoons soy sauce (low-sodium)
- ✓ 1 tablespoon hoisin sauce
- ✓ 1 tablespoon cornstarch
- ✓ 1 tablespoon vegetable oil
- ✓ 2 cloves garlic, minced
- ✓ 1 teaspoon fresh ginger, grated
- ✓ 2 cups mixed vegetables (such as bell peppers, broccoli, carrots, and snow peas), sliced Cooked brown rice or quinoa, for serving

Preparation Steps: In a bowl, combine the soy sauce, hoisin sauce, and cornstarch. Add the sliced lamb to the mixture and toss to coat evenly. Let it marinate for about 10-15 minutes. Heat vegetable oil in a large skillet or wok over medium-high heat. Add the minced garlic and grated ginger, and stir-fry for about 30 seconds until fragrant. Add the marinated lamb to the skillet and stir-fry for 2-3 minutes until browned and cooked through. Add the mixed vegetables to the skillet and continue stir-frying for another 3-4 minutes until the vegetables are tender yet crisp. Serve the lamb and vegetable stir-fry hot over cooked brown rice or quinoa.

Nutritional Info: Calories: 350, Protein: 25g, Carbohydrates: 15g, Fat: 20g, Fiber: 4g

6. Tuna and Brown Rice Bowl

(Setup Time: 10 mins | Cooked in: 20 mins for brown rice)

This recipe combines tuna, a lean source of protein, with brown rice, a whole grain rich in fiber and essential nutrients. It offers a balanced meal for dogs, providing protein, carbohydrates, and healthy fats to support their overall health and well-being.

Recipe Components:
- ✓ 1 cup cooked brown rice
- ✓ 1 can tuna in water, drained
- ✓ 1/2 cup cooked green peas
- ✓ 1 carrot, grated
- ✓ 1 tablespoon olive oil
- ✓ Fresh parsley, chopped (for garnish)

Preparation Steps: In a mixing bowl, combine the cooked brown rice, drained tuna, cooked green peas, and grated carrot. Drizzle olive oil over the mixture. Toss everything together until well combined. Divide the tuna and brown rice mixture into serving bowls. Garnish with chopped fresh parsley before serving.

Nutritional Info: Calories: 300, Protein: 20g, Carbohydrates: 30g, Fat: 10g, Fiber: 5g

7. Pork and Pumpkin Chili

(Setup Time: 15 mins | Cooked in: 45 mins)

This hearty chili recipe features lean pork, nutritious pumpkin, and a blend of flavorful spices. It provides a rich source of protein, vitamins, and antioxidants, making it a satisfying and nutritious meal option for dogs.

Recipe Components:
- ✓ 1 pound lean ground pork
- ✓ 1 can (15 ounces) pumpkin puree
- ✓ 1 can (15 ounces) kidney beans, drained and rinsed
- ✓ 1 can (14.5 ounces) diced tomatoes
- ✓ 1 tablespoon chili powder
- ✓ 1 teaspoon ground cumin
- ✓ Salt and pepper to taste
- ✓ Fresh cilantro, chopped (for garnish)

Preparation Steps: In a large pot or Dutch oven, brown the ground pork over medium heat until cooked through. Stir in the pumpkin puree, diced tomatoes, kidney beans, chili powder, and ground cumin. Season with salt and pepper to taste, and bring the chili to a simmer. Cover and let the chili simmer for about 20-25 minutes, stirring occasionally. Once the chili is heated through and the flavors are well combined, remove from heat. Serve the pork and pumpkin chili hot, garnished with chopped fresh cilantro.

Nutritional Info: Calories: 350, Protein: 25g, Carbohydrates: 30g, Fat: 15g, Fiber: 8g

8. Venison and Lentil Soup

(Setup Time: 15 mins | Cooked in: 60 mins)

This hearty soup combines venison, a lean and protein-rich meat, with nutrient-dense lentils to create a wholesome and filling meal for dogs. Packed with vitamins, minerals, and fiber, this soup promotes overall health and provides essential nutrients for your canine companion.

Recipe Components:

- ✓ 1 pound venison stew meat, diced
- ✓ 1 cup dried green lentils
- ✓ 4 cups low-sodium beef broth
- ✓ 2 carrots, diced
- ✓ 2 celery stalks, diced
- ✓ 1 teaspoon dried thyme
- ✓ Pepper to taste
- ✓ Fresh parsley, chopped (for garnish)

Preparation Steps: In a large soup pot, brown the diced venison stew meat over medium heat until evenly browned. Add the diced carrots and celery to the pot, and sauté until vegetables are tender. Pour in the low-sodium beef broth and add the dried green lentils to the pot. Season with dried thyme and pepper to taste. Bring the soup to a boil, then reduce the heat to low and let it simmer for about 45-50 minutes, or until the lentils are tender and the flavors have melded together. Once the soup is cooked through, remove from heat and let it cool slightly. Serve the venison and lentil soup warm, garnished with chopped fresh parsley.

Nutritional Info: Calories: 320, Protein: 30g, Carbohydrates: 25g, Fat: 10g, Fiber: 8g

9. Duck and Potato Hash

(Setup Time: 15 mins | Cooked in: 30 mins)

This duck and potato hash recipe offers a unique blend of flavors and textures, combining tender duck meat with hearty potatoes. Duck is rich in protein and provides essential amino acids, while potatoes offer carbohydrates for energy. Together, they create a satisfying and nutritious meal for dogs.

Recipe Components:

- ✓ 1 pound duck breast, cooked and shredded
- ✓ 2 large potatoes, peeled and diced
- ✓ 1 tablespoon olive oil
- ✓ 1 teaspoon dried rosemary
- ✓ Salt and pepper to taste

- ✓ Fresh chives, chopped (for garnish)

Preparation Steps: In a large skillet, heat olive oil over medium heat. Add the diced potatoes to the skillet and cook until they are tender and lightly browned. Stir in the shredded duck breast and dried rosemary, and continue to cook until the duck is heated through. Season the duck and potato hash with salt and pepper to taste. Once everything is cooked and seasoned to your liking, remove from heat. Serve the duck and potato hash hot, garnished with chopped fresh chives.

Nutritional Info: Calories: 380, Protein: 25g, Carbohydrates: 30g, Fat: 15g, Fiber: 5g

10. Cod and Spinach Bake

(Setup Time: 10 mins | Cooked in: 20 mins)

This cod and spinach bake combines lean cod fish with nutrient-rich spinach to create a flavorful and nutritious meal for dogs. Cod is an excellent source of high-quality protein and essential omega-3 fatty acids, while spinach provides vitamins, minerals, and antioxidants. Together, they offer a well-rounded and satisfying dish for your canine companion.

Recipe Components:

- ✓ 1 pound cod fillets
- ✓ 2 cups fresh spinach, chopped
- ✓ 1 cup low-sodium chicken broth
- ✓ 1 tablespoon olive oil
- ✓ 1 lemon, sliced
- ✓ Pepper to taste
- ✓ Fresh parsley, chopped (for garnish)

Preparation Steps: Preheat your oven to 375°F (190°C). Lightly grease a baking dish with olive oil. Place the cod fillets in the prepared baking dish, and season with salt, and pepper. Arrange the chopped spinach around the cod fillets in the baking dish. Pour the low-sodium chicken broth over the cod and spinach. Drizzle olive oil over the top of the cod and spinach, and garnish with slices of lemon. Cover the baking dish with aluminum foil and bake in the preheated oven for about 20-25 minutes, or until the cod is cooked through and flakes easily with a fork. Once the cod is cooked, remove the baking dish from the oven and let it cool slightly. Serve the cod and spinach bake warm, garnished with chopped fresh parsley.

Nutritional Info: Calories: 220, Protein: 25g, Carbohydrates: 5g, Fat: 10g, Fiber: 2g

11. Rabbit and Carrot Stew

(Setup Time: 15 mins | Cooked in: 30 mins)

Rabbit and carrot stew is a nutritious and flavorful meal suitable for dogs. Rabbit meat is lean and rich in protein, while carrots provide essential vitamins and fiber. This stew is gentle on the digestive system and offers a balanced combination of proteins and vegetables.

Recipe Components:

- ✓ 1 pound rabbit meat, diced
- ✓ 2 cups carrots, chopped
- ✓ 1 tablespoon olive oil
- ✓ 4 cups water or low-sodium broth

Preparation Steps: Heat olive oil in a large pot over medium heat. Add diced rabbit meat and cook until browned. Add chopped carrots and water or broth to the pot. Bring the stew to a boil, then reduce heat and simmer for 20-25 minutes, or until the rabbit is tender. Allow the stew to cool before serving to your dog.

Nutritional Info: Protein: 18g, Fat: 6g, Carbohydrates: 4g, Fiber: 1.5g

12. Sardine and Oatmeal Porridge

(Setup Time: 10 mins | Cooked in: 15 mins)

Sardine and oatmeal porridge is a wholesome and nutritious meal for dogs. Sardines are a great source of omega-3 fatty acids, while oatmeal provides fiber and energy. This porridge is easy to digest and suitable for dogs of all ages.

Recipe Components:

- ✓ 1 cup rolled oats
- ✓ 1 can sardines in water, drained
- ✓ 2 cups water or low-sodium broth

Preparation Steps: In a saucepan, bring water or broth to a boil. Stir in rolled oats and reduce heat to low. Simmer the oats for 10-15 minutes, stirring occasionally, until cooked. Remove the saucepan from heat and allow the oatmeal to cool slightly. Flake the sardines and mix them into the cooked oatmeal. Let the porridge cool completely before serving to your dog.

Nutritional Info: Protein: 12g, Fat: 8g, Carbohydrates: 20g, Fiber: 3g

13. Trout and Carrot Mash

(Setup Time: 10 mins | Cooked in: 15 mins)

Trout and carrot mash is a nutritious and flavorful dish that provides essential nutrients for dogs. Trout is rich in omega-3 fatty acids, while carrots offer vitamins and antioxidants. This mash is easy to prepare and can be served as a standalone meal or mixed with your dog's regular food.

Recipe Components:

- ✓ 1 cup cooked trout, deboned and flaked
- ✓ 1 cup carrots, diced
- ✓ 1/2 cup low-sodium broth or water

Preparation Steps: In a pot, bring water or broth to a boil. Add diced carrots to the pot and cook until tender, about 8-10 minutes. Drain the carrots and transfer them to a mixing bowl. Add the cooked trout to the bowl and mash together with the carrots using a fork or potato masher. Allow the mash to cool before serving it to your dog.

Nutritional Info: Protein: 15g, Fat: 5g, Carbohydrates: 10g, Fiber: 2.5g

14. Beef and Spinach Lasagna

(Setup Time: 20 mins | Cooked in: 40 mins)

Beef and spinach lasagna is a hearty and nutritious meal suitable for dogs. Lean ground beef provides protein, while spinach adds vitamins and minerals. This lasagna is made without pasta, making it a grain-free option for dogs with sensitivities.

Recipe Components:
- 1 pound lean ground beef
- 2 cups fresh spinach, chopped
- 1 cup low-fat cottage cheese
- 1 egg
- 1/4 cup grated Parmesan cheese

Preparation Steps: Preheat your oven to 350°F (175°C). In a skillet, cook the ground beef over medium heat until browned. Drain any excess fat. In a mixing bowl, combine the cooked ground beef, chopped spinach, cottage cheese, egg, and grated Parmesan cheese. Spread the mixture evenly in a greased baking dish. Bake the lasagna in the preheated oven for 30-35 minutes, or until set and golden brown on top. Allow the lasagna to cool before slicing it into portions for your dog.

Nutritional Info: Protein: 20g, Fat: 8g, Carbohydrates: 5g, Fiber: 1.5g

13. Trout and Carrot Mash

(Setup Time: 10 mins | Cooked in: 15 mins)

Trout and carrot mash is a nutritious and flavorful dish that provides essential nutrients for dogs. Trout is rich in omega-3 fatty acids, while carrots offer vitamins and antioxidants. This mash is easy to prepare and can be served as a standalone meal or mixed with your dog's regular food.

Recipe Components:
- 1 cup cooked trout, deboned and flaked
- 1 cup carrots, diced
- 1/2 cup low-sodium broth or water

Preparation Steps: In a pot, bring water or broth to a boil. Add diced carrots to the pot and cook until tender, about 8-10 minutes. Drain the carrots and transfer them to a mixing bowl. Add the cooked trout to the bowl and mash together with the carrots using a fork or potato masher. Allow the mash to cool before serving it to your dog.

Nutritional Info: Protein: 15g, Fat: 5g, Carbohydrates: 10g, Fiber: 2.5g

15. Pork and Apple Stew

(Setup Time: 15 mins | Cooked in: 30 mins)

Pork and apple stew is a delicious and nutritious meal that dogs will love. Pork provides protein, while apples offer vitamins and natural sweetness. This stew is easy to digest and can be served as a comforting meal for dogs of all sizes.

Recipe Components:
- 1 pound pork loin, diced
- 2 apples, cored and diced
- 1 cup green beans, chopped
- 2 cups low-sodium chicken broth
- 1 tablespoon olive oil

Preparation Steps: In a large pot, heat olive oil over medium heat. Add diced pork loin to the pot and cook until browned on all sides. Add diced apples and chopped green beans to the pot and sauté for a few minutes. Pour in low-sodium chicken broth and bring the mixture to a simmer. Cover the pot and let the stew cook for about 20-25 minutes, or until the pork is cooked through and the apples are tender. Remove the pot from the heat and allow the stew to cool before serving it to your dog.

Nutritional Info: Protein: 18g, Fat: 6g, Carbohydrates: 8g, Fiber: 2.5g

13. Trout and Carrot Mash

(Setup Time: 10 mins | Cooked in: 15 mins)

Trout and carrot mash is a nutritious and flavorful dish that provides essential nutrients for dogs. Trout is rich in omega-3 fatty acids, while carrots offer vitamins and antioxidants. This mash is easy to prepare and can be served as a standalone meal or mixed with your dog's regular food.

Recipe Components:
- 1 cup cooked trout, deboned and flaked
- 1 cup carrots, diced
- 1/2 cup low-sodium broth or water

Preparation Steps: In a pot, bring water or broth to a boil. Add diced carrots to the pot and cook until tender, about 8-10 minutes. Drain the carrots and transfer them to a mixing bowl.

Add the cooked trout to the bowl and mash together with the carrots using a fork or potato masher. Allow the mash to cool before serving it to your dog.

Nutritional Info: Protein: 15g, Fat: 5g, Carbohydrates: 10g, Fiber: 2.5g

16. Turkey and Cranberry Meatballs

(Setup Time: 15 mins | Cooked in: 20 mins)

These turkey and cranberry meatballs are a flavorful and nutritious option for your canine companion. Turkey provides lean protein, while cranberries offer antioxidants and a tangy flavor that dogs enjoy. This dish is rich in essential nutrients and is sure to be a hit with your furry friend.

Recipe Components:

- ✓ 1 pound ground turkey
- ✓ 1/2 cup dried cranberries, finely chopped
- ✓ 1/4 cup oats
- ✓ 1 egg
- ✓ 1 tablespoon olive oil

Preparation Steps: Preheat oven to 375°F (190°C) and line a baking sheet with parchment paper. In a large bowl, combine ground turkey, chopped cranberries, oats, egg, and olive oil. Mix until well combined. Roll the mixture into small meatballs and place them on the prepared baking sheet. Bake for 20 minutes or until cooked through. Allow to cool before serving to your dog. **Nutritional Info:** Calories: 50, Protein: 6g, Fat: 2.5g, Carbohydrates: 2g, Fiber: 0.5g

17. Salmon and Pumpkin Pasta

(Setup Time: 20 mins | Cooked in: 15 mins)

This salmon and pumpkin pasta is a wholesome meal packed with omega-3 fatty acids from salmon and fiber-rich pumpkin. The combination of flavors is sure to tantalize your dog's taste buds while providing essential nutrients for their health and well-being.

Recipe Components:

- ✓ 1 cup cooked salmon, flaked
- ✓ 1/2 cup pumpkin puree
- ✓ 1 cup cooked pasta (without seasoning)
- ✓ 1 tablespoon olive oil
- ✓ Parsley (optional, for garnish)

Preparation Steps: In a skillet, heat olive oil over medium heat. Add flaked salmon and pumpkin puree, stirring until heated through. Add cooked pasta to the skillet, tossing until well coated with the salmon and pumpkin mixture.

Cook for an additional 2-3 minutes, allowing the flavors to meld. Remove from heat and garnish with parsley if desired. Allow to cool before serving to your dog.

Nutritional Info: Calories: 150, Protein: 10g, Fat: 5g, Carbohydrates: 15g, Fiber: 2g

18. Duck and Blueberry Bake

(Setup Time: 25 mins | Cooked in: 30 mins)

This duck and blueberry bake is a delicious and nutritious meal for your dog. Duck provides a flavorful source of protein, while blueberries add antioxidants and a hint of sweetness. This dish is sure to please even the pickiest of eaters.

Recipe Components:

- ✓ 1 cup cooked duck meat, shredded
- ✓ 1/2 cup blueberries
- ✓ 1/4 cup oat flour
- ✓ 1 egg
- ✓ 1/4 cup low-sodium chicken broth

Preparation Steps: Preheat oven to 350°F (175°C) and grease a baking dish. In a large bowl, combine shredded duck meat, blueberries, oat flour, egg, and chicken broth. Mix until well combined. Transfer the mixture to the prepared baking dish and spread it evenly. Bake for 30 minutes or until the top is golden brown and the bake is set. Allow to cool before serving to your dog.

Nutritional Info: Calories: 200, Protein: 15g, Fat: 8g, Carbohydrates: 15g, Fiber: 3g

19. Chicken and Chickpea Curry

(Setup Time: 20 mins | Cooked in: 25 mins)

This chicken and chickpea curry is a hearty and flavorful dish that your dog will love. Chicken provides lean protein, while chickpeas add fiber and texture. The mild spices used in this curry provide a delicious aroma and taste without being overwhelming for your furry friend.

Recipe Components:

- ✓ 1 cup cooked chicken breast, diced
- ✓ 1/2 cup cooked chickpeas
- ✓ 1/4 cup coconut milk
- ✓ 1/4 cup low-sodium chicken broth
- ✓ 1/4 teaspoon turmeric
- ✓ 1/4 teaspoon ginger
- ✓ 1/4 teaspoon cinnamon

- ✓ 1 tablespoon olive oil

Preparation Steps: In a skillet, heat olive oil over medium heat. Add diced chicken breast to the skillet and cook until lightly browned. Add cooked chickpeas, coconut milk, chicken broth, turmeric, ginger, and cinnamon to the skillet. Stir well to combine. Simmer the mixture for about 15-20 minutes, allowing the flavors to meld together and the sauce to thicken. Once the curry reaches the desired consistency, remove it from heat and let it cool slightly before serving to your dog.

Nutritional Info: Cal: 180 kcal, Protein: 16g, Fat: 8g, Carb: 10g, Fiber: 3g, Calcium: 20mg, Iron: 1mg

20. Trout and Couscous Salad

(Setup Time: 15 mins | Cooked in: 15 mins)

Trout and couscous salad is a refreshing and nutritious option for your canine companion. Trout provides lean protein and omega-3 fatty acids, while couscous offers carbohydrates and fiber. The addition of vegetables adds vitamins and minerals to this flavorful salad.

Recipe Components:
- ✓ 1 cup cooked chicken breast, diced
- ✓ 1 cup cooked trout, flaked
- ✓ 1/2 cup cooked whole wheat couscous
- ✓ 1/4 cup diced cucumber
- ✓ 1/4 cup diced tomato
- ✓ 1/4 cup shredded carrots
- ✓ 1 tablespoon chopped parsley
- ✓ 1 tablespoon olive oil
- ✓ 1 tablespoon lemon juice

Preparation Steps: In a large bowl, combine cooked trout, cooked whole wheat couscous, diced cucumber, diced tomato, shredded carrots, and chopped parsley. Drizzle olive oil and lemon juice over the salad ingredients. Toss the salad gently until all ingredients are well mixed. Serve the trout and couscous salad immediately to your dog or refrigerate it for later use.

Nutritional Info: Calories: 150 kcal, Protein: 15g, Fat: 6g, Carbohydrates: 10g Fiber: 2g, Calcium: 20mg, Iron: 1mg

5.4 Canine First Aid: Basic Emergency Care for Dogs

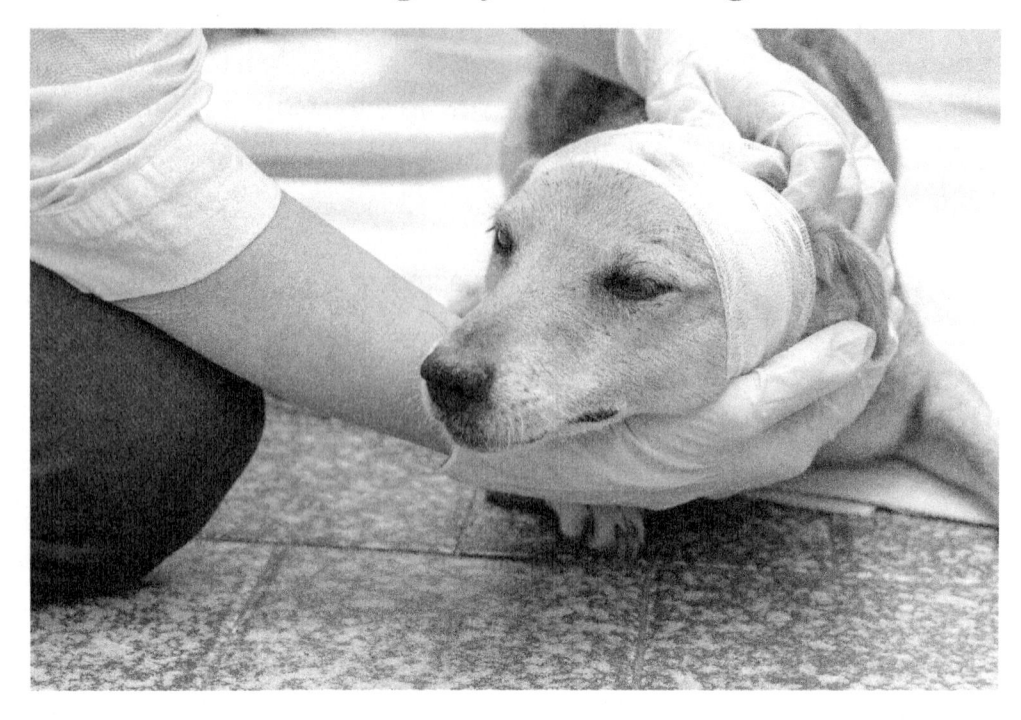

1. Identifying Common Health Emergencies

Identifying common health emergencies in dogs is crucial for pet owners to provide timely and appropriate care. Being able to recognize the signs and symptoms of these emergencies can make a significant difference in the outcome for your furry friend. In the event of an emergency, it's essential to remain calm, assess the situation, and seek veterinary assistance as soon as possible. Early intervention can greatly improve the prognosis for your beloved canine companion.

Here are some of the most common health emergencies in dogs:

✓ **Trauma and Injuries:** Dogs are naturally curious and adventurous animals, which can sometimes lead to accidents and injuries. Common traumatic injuries include cuts, lacerations, fractures, and burns. Signs of trauma may include bleeding, limping, swelling, and visible wounds.

✓ **Choking:** Dogs, especially those prone to scavenging, may accidentally inhale or swallow objects that can become lodged in their throat, leading to choking. Signs of choking include difficulty breathing, excessive drooling, pawing at the mouth, and panic.

✓ **Gastric Dilatation-Volvulus (GDV):** Also known as bloat, GDV is a life-threatening condition in which the stomach fills with gas and twists on itself. This can lead to a rapid onset of symptoms, including abdominal distension, retching without producing vomit, restlessness, and difficulty breathing.

✓ **Heatstroke:** Dogs are susceptible to heatstroke, especially in hot and humid climates or when left in a parked car. Signs of heatstroke include excessive panting, drooling, rapid heart rate, weakness, collapse, and seizures.

✓ **Poisoning:** Dogs can accidentally ingest toxic substances such as medications, household chemicals, plants, and certain human foods. Symptoms of poisoning vary depending on the toxin but may include vomiting, diarrhea, lethargy, seizures, and collapse.

✓ **Respiratory Emergencies:** Respiratory emergencies in dogs can be caused by various factors, including choking, allergic reactions, respiratory infections, and respiratory distress syndrome. Signs of respiratory emergencies include difficulty breathing, wheezing, coughing, and blue-tinged gums.

✓ **Seizures:** Seizures in dogs can be caused by epilepsy, brain tumors, toxins, or metabolic disorders. During a seizure, a dog may experience convulsions, loss of consciousness, drooling, paddling movements, and urination or defecation.

✓ **Allergic Reactions:** Dogs can develop allergic reactions to insect bites, medications, vaccinations, or certain foods. Signs of an allergic reaction may include itching, hives, facial swelling, difficulty breathing, vomiting, diarrhea, and collapse.

✓ **Eye Injuries:** Eye injuries in dogs can occur due to trauma, foreign objects, infections, or underlying medical conditions. Signs of eye injuries may include redness, swelling, discharge, squinting, pawing at the eye, and reluctance to open the affected eye.

✓ **Gastrointestinal Issues:** Dogs may experience gastrointestinal emergencies such as gastric dilatation-volvulus (bloat), intestinal blockages, pancreatitis, and hemorrhagic gastroenteritis. Symptoms include vomiting, diarrhea, abdominal pain, bloating, and lethargy.

✓ **Anaphylaxis:** Anaphylaxis is a severe and potentially life-threatening allergic reaction that can occur rapidly after exposure to an allergen. In dogs, it can be caused by insect stings, medications, vaccines, or food allergens. Symptoms include swelling of the face, difficulty breathing, vomiting, diarrhea, shock, and loss of consciousness.

✓ **Diabetic Emergencies:** Diabetic dogs may experience diabetes-related emergencies such as hypoglycemia (low blood sugar) or diabetic ketoacidosis (a severe complication of diabetes). Symptoms include lethargy, weakness, tremors, confusion, loss of coordination, and seizures.

✓ **Heat Exhaustion:** Heat exhaustion is a less severe condition than heatstroke but can still be dangerous for dogs. Symptoms include fatigue, shortness of breath, weakness, excessive panting, nausea, and increased salivation.

✓ **Frostbite:** Frostbite can occur when dogs are exposed to extremely cold temperatures for prolonged periods. Extremities such as ears, paws, and tails are particularly at risk. Symptoms include pale, cold, and hard skin, pain, swelling, and blisters.

✓ **Hypoglycemia in Puppies:** Puppies can experience episodes of hypoglycemia due to their liver's inability to maintain blood sugar levels during prolonged fasting. Symptoms include weakness, tremors, confusion, seizures, and loss of consciousness.

2. Creating a First Aid Kit for Dogs

A well-equipped first aid kit is essential for addressing minor injuries and managing emergencies in dogs. Here's a comprehensive list of items to include in your canine first aid kit:

- ✓ **Storage Container:** Begin with a durable and waterproof container to store all the supplies. Consider a portable and easily accessible container that can be kept at home and taken on outings.

- ✓ **Emergency Contact Information:** Include a laminated card with essential contact information, including your veterinarian's phone number, the nearest emergency veterinary clinic, and poison control hotline numbers.

- ✓ **Medical Records:** Keep copies of your dog's medical records, including vaccination records, recent medications, and any relevant health history, in a waterproof bag or container.

- ✓ **Bandages and Gauze:** Include a variety of bandages, sterile gauze pads, and adhesive tape for wrapping wounds and controlling bleeding. Non-stick pads are preferable to avoid sticking to the wound.

- ✓ **Antiseptic Wipes and Solutions:** Pack antiseptic wipes or solutions such as chlorhexidine or povidone-iodine for cleaning wounds and preventing infection.

- ✓ **Hydrogen Peroxide:** Hydrogen peroxide can be used to induce vomiting in dogs in cases of ingestion of certain toxins. However, always consult with a veterinarian or poison control center before administering hydrogen peroxide.

- ✓ **Sterile Saline Solution:** Saline solution is useful for flushing out wounds, eyes, and ears. Ensure it is sterile and free of additives or preservatives.

- ✓ **Tweezers and Scissors:** Include tweezers for removing splinters, ticks, or debris from your dog's skin. Additionally, pack blunt-ended scissors for cutting bandages and gauze.

- ✓ **Digital Thermometer:** A digital thermometer specifically designed for dogs can help monitor your dog's temperature in case of fever or heatstroke. Avoid using glass thermometers.

- ✓ **Tick Removal Tool:** Pack a tick removal tool or tick twister for safely and effectively removing ticks from your dog's skin to reduce the risk of tick-borne diseases.

- ✓ **Emergency Blanket:** Include a compact emergency blanket to help keep your dog warm and prevent hypothermia in case of injury or shock.

- ✓ **Muzzle or Fabric Strips:** In stressful situations, even the gentlest dog may become frightened or defensive, posing a risk to anyone trying to provide assistance. Pack a properly fitting muzzle or fabric strips to prevent biting.

- ✓ **Latex Gloves:** Latex or nitrile gloves are essential for protecting yourself from bodily fluids and preventing cross-contamination during first aid procedures.

✓ **Styptic Powder or Gel:** In the event of a nail trim gone wrong, styptic powder or gel can help quickly stop bleeding from a torn nail.

✓ **Emergency Treats:** Pack a supply of your dog's favorite treats to help keep them calm and distracted during first aid procedures or emergencies.

✓ **Medications:** Canine-specific pain relievers such as buffered aspirin (under veterinary guidance), antihistamine for allergic reactions (e.g., Benadryl), activated charcoal to absorb ingested toxins (use as directed by a veterinarian), and any prescription medications your dog requires regularly. Consult with your veterinarian to include any emergency medications prescribed for your dog, such as antihistamines for allergic reactions or medications for managing chronic conditions.

✓ **Emergency Food and Water:** Include a small supply of your dog's regular food and bottled water in case of extended emergencies or travel situations.

✓ **Flashlight:** A compact flashlight or headlamp with extra batteries can be invaluable for examining your dog in low-light conditions or during nighttime emergencies.

✓ **Basic First Aid Manual:** Include a basic first aid manual or reference guide specifically tailored to pet emergencies to provide guidance in stressful situations.

✓ **Personalized Items:** Copies of your dog's medical records, including vaccination history and any relevant health information, a recent photo of your dog for identification purposes in case of separation, and any specific items recommended by your veterinarian based on your dog's health condition or medical history.

✓ **Personal Protective Equipment:** Consider adding personal protective equipment such as a face shield or safety goggles for your safety during first aid procedures.

Regularly check and update your canine first aid kit to ensure that all supplies are in good condition, within expiration dates, and tailored to your dog's specific needs. Store the kit in a readily accessible location, and familiarize yourself with its contents and their proper use to be prepared for any unexpected health emergencies that may arise with your furry companion.

3. Basic First Aid Techniques for Dogs

When your canine companion experiences an injury or sudden illness, knowing how to administer basic first aid can make a significant difference in their outcome. Remember that while first aid is essential, it is not a substitute for professional veterinary care. Always seek veterinary attention for serious injuries or illnesses to ensure the best possible outcome for your dog's health and well-being.

Here are essential first aid techniques every dog owner should know:

✓ **Assess the Situation:** Before administering any first aid, assess the situation to ensure your safety and your dog's safety. Remove any potential hazards or sources of danger, such as traffic or aggressive animals.

✓ **Stay Calm:** Dogs can sense their owners' emotions, so it's crucial to remain calm and composed during a crisis. Your calm demeanor can help keep your dog relaxed and cooperative during first aid procedures.

✓ **Approach with Caution:** Even the friendliest dogs may become frightened or defensive when injured or in pain. Approach your dog slowly and cautiously, speaking to them in a calm and reassuring tone to avoid escalating their stress levels.

✓ **Control Bleeding:** If your dog is bleeding, apply direct pressure to the wound using a clean cloth or bandage. Elevate the injured area if possible and maintain pressure until the bleeding stops or help arrives. Avoid using tourniquets unless absolutely necessary, as they can cause tissue damage.

✓ **Stabilize Fractures:** If you suspect your dog has a fracture, avoid manipulating the injured limb and instead stabilize it to prevent further damage. Use a splint or makeshift support to immobilize the limb before transporting your dog to the vet.

✓ **Manage Choking:** If your dog is choking, carefully open their mouth and check for any obstructions. If you can see and safely remove the object, do so with caution. If the object is lodged deep in the throat or your dog is unconscious, perform modified versions of the Heimlich maneuver by delivering quick, upward thrusts to the abdomen.

✓ **Perform CPR:** Cardiopulmonary resuscitation (CPR) can be lifesaving in cases of cardiac arrest or respiratory failure. If your dog is unresponsive and not breathing, lay them on their side and perform chest compressions and rescue breaths following the guidelines recommended by veterinary professionals.

✓ **Address Burns and Heatstroke:** For burns, gently flush the affected area with cool water and cover with a clean, dry bandage. In cases of heatstroke, move your dog to a cool, shaded area, apply cool water or ice packs to their body, and seek veterinary attention immediately.

✓ **Handle Seizures:** During a seizure, keep your dog away from sharp objects or furniture that could cause injury. Place a soft blanket or cushion beneath their head to prevent trauma, and time the duration of the seizure. Contact your veterinarian if seizures last longer than a few minutes or occur frequently.

✓ **Administer Medications:** If your dog requires emergency medications, such as antihistamines for allergic reactions or pain relievers for acute pain, follow your veterinarian's instructions carefully. Be sure to monitor your dog closely for any adverse reactions or side effects.

✓ **Managing Allergic Reactions:** If your dog exhibits signs of an allergic reaction, such as facial swelling, hives, or difficulty breathing, administer an antihistamine if recommended by your veterinarian. Keep your dog calm and monitor their condition closely until veterinary help is available.

✓ **Treating Eye Injuries:** If your dog sustains an eye injury, avoid touching or applying pressure to the affected eye. Flush the eye gently with saline solution to remove any debris or foreign objects. Cover the injured eye with a clean, moistened bandage and seek veterinary care promptly.

✓ **Dealing with Bee Stings or Insect Bites:** If your dog is stung by a bee or bitten by an insect, remove the stinger if visible using a scraping motion with a credit card or similar object. Apply a cold compress or ice pack to reduce swelling and discomfort. Monitor your dog for signs of an allergic reaction and seek veterinary attention if necessary.

✓ **Addressing Gastric Distress:** In cases of gastric distress, such as vomiting or diarrhea, withhold food for 12-24 hours to allow your dog's digestive system to rest. Offer small amounts of water frequently to prevent dehydration. If symptoms persist or worsen, consult your veterinarian for further guidance on when to reintroduce food and how to manage ongoing gastrointestinal issues.

✓ **Recognizing Signs of Shock:** Shock is a life-threatening condition that requires immediate attention. Signs of shock in dogs include pale gums, rapid heartbeat, shallow breathing, and weakness. Keep your dog warm and elevate their hindquarters slightly to improve circulation while seeking urgent veterinary care.

✓ **Managing Severe Bleeding:** In cases of severe bleeding that cannot be controlled with direct pressure, apply a tourniquet above the wound if possible. Use a fabric strip or belt to apply steady pressure to the limb, avoiding excessive tightness. Seek immediate veterinary assistance as tourniquets should only be used as a last resort.

✓ **Transporting Injured Dogs:** When transporting an injured dog, use a sturdy, flat surface such as a stretcher, board, or folded blanket to minimize movement and support their body. Avoid bending or twisting their spine and secure them safely in a vehicle for transportation to the nearest veterinary facility.

✓ **Monitoring Vital Signs:** Learn how to assess your dog's vital signs, including heart rate, respiratory rate, and temperature. Regularly monitor these parameters at home to establish baseline values and detect any abnormalities early on.

✓ **Administering Subcutaneous Fluids:** In cases of dehydration or fluid loss, your veterinarian may prescribe subcutaneous fluid therapy for your dog. Learn how to safely administer fluids under the skin using a syringe and needle, following your veterinarian's instructions carefully.

✓ **Providing Emotional Support:** Dogs can experience fear, anxiety, and stress during emergencies or medical procedures. Offer reassurance and comfort to your dog through gentle petting, soothing words, and familiar toys or blankets to help alleviate their distress.

It's crucial to familiarize yourself with these basic first aid techniques and regularly practice them to ensure readiness in the event of an emergency. Additionally, consider enrolling in a pet first aid and CPR course to gain hands-on experience and further enhance your skills in providing essential care for your furry friend.

4. Handling Injuries and Wounds

Handling injuries and wounds in your dog requires swift action and careful attention to ensure their well-being. The first step is to evaluate the extent of the injury and the surrounding environment to ensure safety for both you and your dog. Remove any potential hazards and approach your dog calmly and reassuringly. This helps to keep them relaxed and cooperative during the first aid process. If your dog is bleeding, it's essential to control it promptly. Apply direct pressure to the wound using a clean cloth or bandage, and elevate the injured area if possible to reduce blood flow. Severe bleeding may require immediate veterinary attention. Once bleeding is under control, gently clean the wound with mild soap and warm water or a veterinary-approved antiseptic solution. Avoid using harsh substances like hydrogen peroxide or alcohol, as they can irritate the skin. After cleaning, apply a thin layer of antibiotic ointment to the wound to help prevent infection and promote healing. Cover the wound with a sterile gauze pad and secure it in place with adhesive tape or a self-adhesive bandage wrap if necessary. Ensure that the bandage is snug but not too tight, as this can impede blood flow. It's essential to monitor the wound closely for any signs of infection, such as increased redness, swelling, warmth, or discharge. If you notice any concerning symptoms, consult your veterinarian promptly for further guidance. Dogs may instinctively try to lick or chew at their wounds, which can delay healing and introduce bacteria. To prevent this, consider using an Elizabethan collar or deterrent sprays to discourage your dog from interfering with the healing process. While basic first aid can address minor wounds, it's crucial to seek veterinary care for more severe injuries or wounds that show signs of infection or fail to heal. Your veterinarian can assess the extent of the injury and provide appropriate treatment, such as sutures or antibiotics. Finally, ensure that your dog has a comfortable and quiet space to rest while they heal. Monitor their appetite, activity level, and overall demeanor for any changes that may indicate complications.

5. Dealing with Choking and Breathing Difficulties

As we briefly discussed earlier, dealing with choking and breathing difficulties in dogs requires swift and decisive action to prevent further complications. Now, let's delve into this topic in more detail to equip you with the knowledge and skills necessary to handle such emergencies effectively. Choking occurs when an object becomes lodged in your dog's throat, obstructing their airway and making it difficult for them to breathe. Common choking hazards include small toys, bones, balls, or even food items like rawhide chews or chunks of meat. When faced with a choking dog, it's essential to remain calm and act quickly. Start by carefully opening your dog's mouth and inspecting for any visible obstructions. If you can safely remove the object using your fingers or tweezers, do so with caution to avoid pushing it further down the throat. However, if the object is lodged deep in the throat or your dog is unconscious, attempting to remove it manually may cause more harm than good. In such cases, you'll need to perform modified versions of the Heimlich maneuver to dislodge the obstruction and restore airflow.

To perform the Heimlich maneuver on a dog, follow these steps:

- ✓ Stand or kneel behind your dog and wrap your arms around their waist.
- ✓ Make a fist with one hand and place it just behind your dog's ribcage.
- ✓ With your other hand, grasp your fist and give a quick, upward thrust to the abdomen.
- ✓ Repeat the thrusts several times, checking between each attempt to see if the object has been dislodged.
- ✓ If your dog remains unconscious or unable to breathe, continue performing CPR until help arrives.

It's essential to note that the Heimlich maneuver should only be used in cases of severe choking where the dog is unable to breathe or loses consciousness. If your dog is still conscious and able to cough or gag, encourage them to do so to try and dislodge the object themselves. After successfully removing the obstruction or if your dog's breathing becomes labored for any reason, monitor their condition closely and seek veterinary attention as soon as possible. Even if you've managed to clear the airway, there may still be underlying issues that require professional evaluation and treatment.

6. Recognizing Signs of Poisoning

Poisoning is a serious concern for dog owners, as many common household items and substances can be toxic to dogs if ingested, inhaled, or absorbed through the skin. Recognizing the signs of poisoning is crucial for prompt intervention and treatment.

Symptoms. The symptoms of poisoning in dogs can vary depending on the type of toxin involved and the amount ingested. However, common signs of poisoning may include:

- ➢ Vomiting
- ➢ Diarrhea
- ➢ Excessive drooling
- ➢ Difficulty breathing
- ➢ Lethargy or weakness
- ➢ Seizures
- ➢ Loss of appetite
- ➢ Uncoordinated movements
- ➢ Tremors or shaking
- ➢ Pale gums
- ➢ Jaundice (yellowing of the skin or eyes)
- ➢ Collapse or coma

Common Poisons. Dogs can be poisoned by a wide range of substances found in and around the home, including:

- ➢ Human medications (e.g., painkillers, antidepressants, cold medications)
- ➢ Household cleaners and chemicals (e.g., bleach, ammonia, drain cleaners)
- ➢ Certain foods toxic to dogs (e.g., chocolate, grapes, xylitol)
- ➢ Toxic plants and flowers (e.g., lilies, azaleas, tulips)

- Rodenticides and insecticides
- Automotive products (e.g., antifreeze, motor oil)
- Outdoor toxins (e.g., snail bait, fertilizers, mulch)

Immediate Action. If you suspect your dog has ingested a poisonous substance, seek veterinary attention immediately, even if they are not yet showing symptoms. Time is of the essence when it comes to treating poisoning, and delaying treatment could result in serious complications or even death.

Contact Poison Control. In addition to seeking veterinary care, contact a poison control hotline or animal poison control center for guidance on how to proceed. They can provide valuable information on the specific toxin involved and recommend appropriate first aid measures or treatment options.

Prevention. The best way to deal with poisoning is to prevent it from happening in the first place. Keep potentially toxic substances out of your dog's reach, secure garbage cans, avoid feeding your dog human foods that are harmful to them, and familiarize yourself with common household toxins.

7. Managing Heatstroke and Hypothermia

Heatstroke and hypothermia are serious conditions that can pose significant risks to your dog's health, especially during extreme weather conditions. Heatstroke occurs when a dog's body temperature rises to dangerously high levels, usually due to prolonged exposure to high temperatures or physical exertion in hot weather. Brachycephalic breeds, elderly dogs, and those with pre-existing health conditions are particularly vulnerable.

Common signs of heatstroke in dogs include:

- Excessive panting
- Rapid breathing
- Bright red gums and tongue
- Thick, sticky saliva
- Vomiting
- Diarrhea
- Weakness or collapse
- Seizures

If you suspect your dog is suffering from heatstroke, take immediate action to cool them down:

- Move your dog to a shaded or air-conditioned area.
- Offer cool, not cold, water to drink.
- Wet your dog's fur with cool water and use fans or air conditioning to aid evaporation.
- Place cool, wet towels over your dog's body, focusing on the groin, armpits, and neck.
- Monitor their body temperature and seek veterinary attention promptly.

Hypothermia occurs when a dog's body temperature drops below normal levels, typically due to exposure to cold temperatures, wet conditions, or submersion in cold water. Small breeds, thin-coated dogs, and those with certain medical conditions are at higher risk.

Signs of hypothermia in dogs may include:

- Shivering
- Cold or pale skin
- Weakness or lethargy
- Slowed heart rate and breathing
- Stiff muscles
- Confusion or disorientation
- Collapse

If you suspect your dog is suffering from hypothermia, take immediate steps to warm them up:

- Move your dog to a warm, dry area indoors.
- Wrap them in dry blankets or towels.
- Provide warm fluids to drink, but avoid giving them alcohol.
- Use heating pads or warm water bottles wrapped in towels to gently warm your dog's body, focusing on the abdomen, armpits, and groin.
- Monitor their body temperature and seek veterinary attention promptly.

8. Responding to Seizures

Witnessing your dog experiencing a seizure can be distressing, but understanding how to respond calmly and effectively can help minimize the impact and ensure your dog's safety. Seizures in dogs can vary in severity and duration, and while they can be alarming to witness, most seizures are not life-threatening. Move your dog away from any potential hazards or sharp objects that could cause injury during the seizure. Clear the surrounding area to create a safe space for your dog to convulse without risk of harm. Note the start time of the seizure and monitor its duration. Most seizures in dogs last between 1 to 3 minutes, but some may be shorter or longer. If the seizure lasts longer than 5 minutes or if your dog has multiple seizures in a short period, seek veterinary attention immediately. Avoid restraining your dog or attempting to hold them down during the seizure. This can cause injury to both you and your dog and may prolong the seizure. Place a soft blanket or cushion beneath your dog's head to protect them from hitting their head on the floor during convulsions. Do not attempt to force anything into your dog's mouth or hold their tongue during the seizure, as this can cause injury. While your dog is experiencing a seizure, observe their behavior closely and offer reassurance in a calm and soothing voice. Avoid hovering over them or making sudden movements that could startle them. After the seizure ends, allow your dog to rest in a quiet, comfortable area. Keep them warm and monitor their condition closely for any signs of distress or further seizures. If your dog experiences their first seizure or if seizures become more frequent or severe, contact your veterinarian for further evaluation and guidance. Your vet may recommend diagnostic tests to determine the underlying cause of the seizures and develop an appropriate treatment plan.

Keep a record of your dog's seizures, including the date, duration, and any observed triggers or symptoms. This information can help your veterinarian assess your dog's condition and adjust their treatment plan accordingly.

9. Providing CPR for Dogs

CPR, or cardiopulmonary resuscitation, can be a lifesaving measure in cases of cardiac arrest or respiratory failure in dogs. While it's crucial to seek veterinary attention as soon as possible during emergencies, knowing how to perform CPR on your dog can help sustain their vital functions until professional help arrives. As mentioned briefly earlier, CPR involves a combination of chest compressions to stimulate the heart and rescue breaths to provide oxygen to the lungs. Before attempting CPR, ensure that the area is safe and free from hazards, and check your dog's responsiveness by gently tapping or calling their name.

If your dog is unresponsive and not breathing, follow these steps to perform CPR:

➢ **Positioning:** Lay your dog on their right side on a flat, firm surface. Extend their head and neck to open the airway, and gently tilt their head back to straighten the throat.

➢ **Assess Breathing:** Check for signs of breathing by looking for chest movement, listening for breath sounds, and feeling for airflow from the nostrils. If your dog is not breathing, proceed with CPR.

➢ **Perform Chest Compressions:** Place one hand over the widest part of your dog's ribcage, near the heart. For medium to large dogs, use both hands stacked on top of each other. For small dogs or puppies, one hand may be sufficient. Press down firmly and smoothly on the chest, allowing it to recoil completely between compressions. Aim for a rate of 100-120 compressions per minute.

➢ **Provide Rescue Breaths:** After every 30 chest compressions, provide two rescue breaths to your dog. Close your dog's mouth and gently blow into their nostrils until you see their chest rise. Ensure that you maintain a good seal over their muzzle to prevent air from escaping.

➢ **Continue CPR:** Repeat cycles of 30 chest compressions followed by two rescue breaths until your dog resumes breathing on their own or until veterinary help arrives. Monitor your dog's vital signs and adjust your technique as needed.

It's essential to remain calm and focused while performing CPR on your dog. Remember that CPR is not a guarantee of survival but can improve the chances of a positive outcome when administered promptly and correctly. Once your dog's breathing and heartbeat have resumed, seek immediate veterinary attention for further evaluation and treatment. Even if your dog appears to recover, it's essential to have them examined by a veterinarian to address any underlying health issues that may have contributed to the emergency.

10. Transporting Injured Dogs Safely to the Vet

Transporting an injured dog to the veterinary clinic safely and efficiently is crucial for ensuring prompt medical attention and the best possible outcome.

While we briefly discussed this topic earlier, let's delve into it more comprehensively now. In emergency situations where your dog requires immediate veterinary care, it's essential to transport them to the clinic safely and without exacerbating their injuries. Here's how you can ensure a safe journey:

> ➤ **Assessment:** Before attempting to move your injured dog, assess their condition carefully. Check for any signs of trauma, bleeding, or fractures, and determine the extent of their injuries. If possible, stabilize any fractures or wounds before transportation.

> ➤ **Preparation:** Prepare a sturdy and flat surface for transporting your dog, such as a stretcher, board, or folded blanket. Avoid using items that could bend or flex, as they may cause further injury to your dog's spine or limbs.

> ➤ **Lifting:** Approach your dog gently and lift them carefully, supporting their body underneath their chest and abdomen. For larger dogs, consider enlisting the help of another person to lift and support them properly. Avoid lifting your dog by their limbs or pulling them by their collar, as this can cause additional pain or injury.

> ➤ **Positioning:** Once lifted, place your dog gently onto the prepared transport surface, ensuring that their body is fully supported and their head and neck are aligned with their spine. Avoid bending or twisting your dog's body during positioning to prevent further injury.

> ➤ **Securing:** If possible, secure your dog to the transport surface using restraints or straps to prevent them from sliding or falling during transportation. However, ensure that the restraints are not too tight and do not restrict your dog's breathing or circulation.

> ➤ **Covering:** If your dog is in shock or experiencing hypothermia, cover them with a blanket or towel to help maintain their body temperature during transportation. Ensure that the covering is lightweight and breathable to prevent overheating.

> ➤ **Monitoring:** While en route to the veterinary clinic, monitor your dog's vital signs, including their breathing, heart rate, and level of consciousness. Stay calm and reassuring to help keep your dog relaxed and minimize stress during the journey.

> ➤ **Communication:** Inform the veterinary clinic of your dog's condition and the nature of their injuries before your arrival, if possible. This allows the clinic to prepare for your dog's arrival and provide prompt assistance upon your arrival.

> ➤ **Direct Route:** Choose the shortest and most direct route to the veterinary clinic to minimize transportation time and reduce stress on your injured dog. Avoid making unnecessary stops or detours that could prolong the journey unnecessarily.

> ➤ **Emergency Facilities:** If your regular veterinary clinic is closed or unavailable, seek out emergency veterinary facilities in your area for immediate assistance. Familiarize yourself with their location and contact information beforehand to expedite the process in case of emergencies.

Chapter 6: Advanced Training and Enrichment

In this chapter, we delve into the realm of advanced training and enrichment for dogs, exploring techniques and activities beyond the basics to further develop their skills and enhance their well-being. From competition to working roles and therapy dog training, we explore various avenues for advancing your dog's training and fostering a deeper bond between you and your canine companion.

6.1 Advancing Beyond Basic Training: Competition, Working, and Therapy Dog Training

As your dog progresses in their training journey, you may find yourself interested in exploring more specialized avenues such as competition, working roles, or therapy dog training. These advanced training paths offer unique opportunities for both you and your dog to further develop your skills and contribute positively to your community.

Competition Training

Competition training encompasses a wide range of activities aimed at preparing your dog to excel in various dog sports and competitions. From agility and obedience trials to rally obedience, flyball, disc dog competitions, and beyond, these events offer exciting opportunities for dogs and their owners to showcase their skills, athleticism, and teamwork.

- ✓ **Agility:** Agility is a dynamic and exhilarating dog sport where dogs navigate through a timed obstacle course, which includes jumps, tunnels, weave poles, A-frames, and other challenges. Training for agility involves teaching your dog to respond quickly and accurately to your commands while navigating the obstacles with speed and agility. It requires a combination of physical fitness, mental focus, and precise communication between you and your dog. Agility training sessions typically include practicing specific obstacle sequences, refining handling techniques, and building confidence and enthusiasm for the course.

- ✓ **Obedience:** Obedience trials assess a dog's ability to perform a series of predefined exercises with precision and reliability. These exercises often include heeling, recalls, stays, retrieves, and scent discrimination, among others. Training for obedience competitions involves teaching your dog to respond promptly to verbal and visual cues, maintain focus and attention in distracting environments, and execute each exercise with precision and enthusiasm. It requires consistent practice, clear communication, and positive reinforcement to shape desired behaviors and eliminate unwanted ones.

- ✓ **Rally Obedience:** Rally obedience combines elements of traditional obedience with the dynamic nature of agility. Dogs and handlers navigate through a course consisting of designated stations, where they perform a series of obedience exercises, such as sits, downs, turns, and heeling patterns. Unlike traditional obedience, handlers are allowed to encourage their dogs verbally and through body language throughout the course. Rally obedience training focuses on building teamwork, communication, and responsiveness while navigating the course with precision and enthusiasm.

- ✓ **Flyball:** Flyball is a high-energy relay race where teams of dogs compete against each other to retrieve a tennis ball from a spring-loaded box, race back over a series of hurdles, and release the ball to the next dog on their team. Training for flyball involves teaching your dog to sprint over the hurdles, trigger the ball release mechanism, and return the ball quickly and reliably. It requires speed, agility, and coordination, as well as strong teamwork and reliable recall skills. Flyball training sessions typically include practicing box turns, building speed and endurance, and perfecting ball retrieves.

- ✓ **Other Dog Sports:** In addition to the aforementioned sports, there are numerous other dog sports and competitions that dogs and their owners can participate in, including disc dog competitions, dock diving, lure coursing, scent work trials, and more. Each sport offers unique challenges and opportunities for dogs to showcase their natural abilities and talents. Training for these sports often involves specialized skills and techniques tailored to the specific requirements of each event.

Working Roles

Dogs have a long history of serving alongside humans in a multitude of working roles, harnessing their natural abilities and instincts to fulfill essential tasks and support various industries and professions. From herding livestock to assisting law enforcement, military personnel, and performing search and rescue missions, dogs have proven themselves to be invaluable partners in a wide range of fields.

- ✓ **Herding and Livestock Management:** One of the earliest and most traditional working roles for dogs is herding and livestock management. Breeds such as Border Collies, Australian Shepherds, and German Shepherds excel in this role, using their innate herding instincts to control and move livestock with precision and efficiency. Training for herding involves teaching dogs to respond to verbal and whistle commands, navigate varied terrain, and anticipate the movements of livestock to maintain order and safety in the herd.

- ✓ **Law Enforcement and Security:** Dogs play crucial roles in law enforcement and security operations, using their keen senses and specialized training to detect drugs, explosives, and other contraband, track suspects, and apprehend individuals. Breeds such as German Shepherds, Belgian Malinois, and Labrador Retrievers are commonly employed in these roles due to their intelligence, obedience, and versatility. Training for law enforcement and security tasks involves rigorous obedience training, scent detection work, agility training, and simulated real-world scenarios to prepare dogs for the demands of their duties.

- ✓ **Search and Rescue:** Search and rescue dogs are trained to locate and assist individuals who are lost, injured, or trapped in various environments, including wilderness areas, disaster zones, and urban settings. These dogs, often referred to as SAR (Search and Rescue) dogs, undergo intensive training to develop skills such as scent detection, tracking, agility, and obedience. Breeds such as German Shepherds, Bloodhounds, and Golden Retrievers are commonly used in search and rescue operations due to their keen sense of smell, endurance, and trainability.

Training for search and rescue missions involves exposing dogs to a variety of environments and scenarios, simulating real-life search scenarios, and building strong bonds between handlers and their canine partners.

- ✓ **Service and Assistance:** Service dogs provide invaluable assistance to individuals with disabilities, helping them navigate daily life and perform essential tasks with greater independence and confidence. These dogs are trained to perform specific tasks tailored to their handler's needs, such as guiding the visually impaired, alerting to seizures, retrieving dropped items, and providing mobility assistance. Breeds such as Labrador Retrievers, Golden Retrievers, and Standard Poodles are commonly used as service dogs due to their intelligence, temperament, and trainability. Training for service and assistance tasks involves teaching dogs a wide range of skills through positive reinforcement, repetition, and consistent practice, as well as acclimating them to various environments and situations they may encounter while working with their handlers.

- ✓ **Other Working Roles:** In addition to the aforementioned roles, dogs serve in various other working capacities, including therapy and emotional support roles, conservation detection (such as detecting endangered species or invasive pests), agricultural tasks (such as pest control or truffle hunting), and more. Each working role requires specialized training tailored to the specific needs and responsibilities of the job, as well as ongoing education and support to ensure dogs remain proficient and effective in their roles.

Therapy Dog Training

Therapy dog training is a specialized form of canine education aimed at preparing dogs to offer comfort, companionship, and emotional support to individuals in hospitals, nursing homes, schools, and other settings where their presence can provide therapeutic benefits. These dogs serve as ambassadors of goodwill, bringing joy and solace to people in need through their gentle demeanor and empathetic nature. Therapy dogs play a crucial role in enhancing the well-being of individuals facing various challenges, including physical illness, mental health issues, emotional distress, and social isolation. Their presence can help reduce stress and anxiety, lower blood pressure, improve mood, and promote feelings of relaxation and happiness. Therapy dogs are often invited into healthcare facilities, educational institutions, and community centers to interact with patients, residents, students, and staff members, offering a welcome distraction from the difficulties they may be facing. Training for therapy dog work focuses on developing specific skills and behaviors that enable dogs to excel in their role as emotional support companions. Key objectives of therapy dog training include:

- ✓ **Socialization:** Therapy dogs must be comfortable and well-adjusted in various environments and around different people, including children, the elderly, and individuals with disabilities. Training emphasizes exposing dogs to diverse social situations, sights, sounds, and smells to build their confidence and

- ✓ **Obedience:** Therapy dogs must exhibit reliable obedience and responsiveness to their handlers' commands, even in distracting or unfamiliar environments. Training involves teaching dogs basic obedience cues such as sit, stay, down, come, and leave it, as well as more advanced commands as needed.

- ✓ **Empathy and Sensitivity:** Therapy dogs must possess a gentle and empathetic disposition, demonstrating an intuitive understanding of human emotions and responding appropriately to individuals' needs. Training focuses on reinforcing positive interactions and teaching dogs to offer comfort and support in a non-intrusive manner.
- ✓ **Handling Unexpected Situations:** Therapy dogs encounter a variety of unexpected situations and stimuli during their visits, ranging from loud noises to sudden movements and unfamiliar environments. Training prepares dogs to remain calm, composed, and focused in the face of these challenges, allowing them to maintain their therapeutic presence and effectiveness.
- ✓ **Boundary Setting:** While therapy dogs are encouraged to interact with individuals in a friendly and affectionate manner, they must also respect personal boundaries and follow guidelines established by their handlers and the facilities they visit. Training teaches dogs to approach people gently, ask for permission before initiating contact, and respect cues indicating a desire for space or privacy.

In many cases, therapy dogs and their handlers undergo certification through recognized therapy dog organizations to ensure they meet established standards of behavior, temperament, and training. Certification may involve passing temperament evaluations, obedience tests, and simulated therapy visits to assess the dog's suitability for therapy work. Additionally, therapy dog teams often engage in continuing education and ongoing training to maintain their skills, stay updated on best practices, and uphold the integrity of the therapy dog profession. In conclusion, therapy dog training plays a vital role in preparing dogs to offer comfort, companionship, and emotional support to individuals in need. Through structured training programs focused on socialization, obedience, empathy, and resilience, therapy dogs become valued members of their communities, bringing joy and healing wherever they go.

6.2 Enhancing Communication and Understanding Between Owner and Dog

In the realm of advanced training and enrichment, fostering effective communication and deepening the bond between owner and dog is paramount. While basic obedience commands form the foundation of communication, advancing beyond these fundamentals requires a nuanced approach that acknowledges the complexity of the human-canine relationship.

Building a Strong Foundation

Effective communication begins with a strong foundation of mutual trust, respect, and understanding between owner and dog. This foundation is cultivated through consistent training, positive reinforcement, and clear communication of expectations. Advanced training techniques focus on refining communication skills, enhancing mutual understanding, and strengthening the bond between owner and dog.

Advanced Training Techniques

Advanced training techniques represent a multifaceted approach to deepening the bond between owners and their canine companions while honing their skills and understanding.

Here's an in-depth exploration of the various components of advanced training:

- ✓ **Body Language and Cues:** Advanced training places a strong emphasis on the subtle nuances of body language exhibited by both dogs and humans. Owners are encouraged to develop keen observational skills, learning to interpret their dog's posture, facial expressions, and movements. By understanding these cues, owners can gain insight into their dog's thoughts, feelings, and intentions, fostering a deeper level of communication and connection. Similarly, dogs learn to recognize and respond to their owner's body language, facilitating more effective collaboration and mutual understanding.

- ✓ **Verbal Commands and Vocabulary:** Building upon basic verbal commands, advanced training introduces a broader vocabulary and refines the precision and clarity of communication between owner and dog. Owners learn to use specific, consistent verbal cues to convey commands, requests, and expectations to their dogs. For example, using commands like "sit-stay" for maintaining a sitting position for an extended period or "heel" for walking calmly by the owner's side. By expanding their repertoire of verbal commands, owners can engage in more nuanced interactions and responses, enhancing the depth of their communication and strengthening the bond with their canine companions.

- ✓ **Non-Verbal Communication:** In addition to verbal commands, advanced training incorporates non-verbal communication techniques such as hand signals, gestures, and facial expressions. These non-verbal cues serve as supplementary communication channels, providing clarity and reinforcement for desired behaviors. Dogs learn to interpret and respond to subtle non-verbal cues from their owners, further solidifying the bond between them and facilitating seamless communication in various environments and situations. For instance, a raised palm can signal "stay," while a downward-pointing index finger can indicate "down."

- ✓ **Advanced Behavioral Concepts:** Advanced training delves into complex behavioral concepts aimed at shaping and refining a dog's behavior. This includes developing skills such as impulse control, frustration tolerance, and emotional regulation. Owners learn strategies for addressing challenging behaviors and promoting desirable responses in their dogs. For example, teaching a dog to control impulses by waiting patiently for a treat or reinforcing calm behavior in stressful situations. By understanding the underlying motivations and emotions driving behavior, owners can tailor training methods to address specific needs and challenges effectively, promoting self-control and resilience in their canine companions.

- ✓ **Interactive Games and Activities:** Enriching the human-canine relationship goes beyond formal training sessions to include interactive games, activities, and enrichment opportunities. These activities provide mental stimulation, physical exercise, and bonding experiences for both owner and dog. Interactive toys, scent work, agility courses, and canine sports are examples of activities that promote engagement, teamwork, and mutual enjoyment.

By incorporating these activities into their routine, owners can strengthen the bond with their dogs while providing opportunities for learning, growth, and shared experiences. For example, playing hide-and-seek with treats encourages dogs to use their sense of smell and problem-solving skills, fostering mental stimulation and reinforcing the bond between owner and dog.

The Power of Positive Reinforcement

Central to advanced training is the principle of positive reinforcement, which involves rewarding desired behaviors to encourage their repetition. By using rewards such as treats, praise, toys, or opportunities for play, owners reinforce the behaviors they want to see more of, creating a positive learning environment for their dogs. Positive reinforcement fosters motivation, engagement, and trust, paving the way for effective communication and harmonious collaboration between owner and dog.

6.3 Managing Time Effectively for Training Sessions

Effectively managing time during advanced training sessions is crucial for maximizing productivity and achieving desired outcomes. Here's an exploration of key strategies to optimize time utilization during advanced training.

- ✓ **Prioritize Training Goals:** Begin by identifying and prioritizing specific training goals based on your dog's individual needs, abilities, and interests. Focus on areas that require improvement or refinement, such as advanced obedience commands, specialized skills for competition or working roles, or addressing specific behavioral challenges. By setting clear and achievable training objectives, you can allocate time more efficiently and track progress effectively.

- ✓ **Break Training Sessions into Manageable Segments:** Divide training sessions into manageable segments to maintain focus and prevent mental fatigue for both you and your dog. Aim for shorter, more frequent sessions rather than prolonged sessions that may lead to frustration or disengagement. Plan breaks between segments to allow for rest, hydration, and mental processing, ensuring that training remains enjoyable and productive for your dog.

- ✓ **Incorporate Variety and Novelty:** Keep training sessions engaging and stimulating by incorporating a variety of exercises, activities, and environments. Introduce novel challenges, such as new commands, obstacles, or distractions, to promote cognitive flexibility and adaptability in your dog. Rotate between different training locations, both indoor and outdoor, to generalize behaviors and reinforce learning in various contexts. Variety not only prevents boredom but also encourages continued motivation and enthusiasm during training.

- ✓ **Focus on Quality over Quantity:** Prioritize the quality of training interactions over the quantity of repetitions or duration of sessions. Maintain a high standard of precision, consistency, and clarity in your communication and reinforcement techniques. Emphasize meaningful engagement, active participation, and positive reinforcement to keep training sessions rewarding and enjoyable for your dog.

Quality training experiences build confidence, trust, and mutual respect between you and your canine companion, fostering a strong foundation for advanced learning and performance.

- ✓ **Incorporate Training into Daily Routine:** Integrate training exercises and activities seamlessly into your daily routine to maximize opportunities for learning and reinforcement. Incorporate obedience commands, impulse control exercises, or interactive games into everyday activities such as mealtime, walks, or play sessions. By weaving training into daily life, you create a consistent and supportive learning environment that reinforces desired behaviors and strengthens the bond between you and your dog. Consistent reinforcement and repetition facilitate long-term retention and application of learned skills in real-world scenarios.

- ✓ **Monitor Progress and Adjust Accordingly:** Regularly assess your dog's progress and adjust your training approach as needed to address evolving needs and challenges. Keep detailed records of training sessions, noting successes, setbacks, and areas for improvement. Celebrate achievements and milestones along the way, while also recognizing opportunities for growth and refinement. Remain flexible and adaptable in your training methods, experimenting with different techniques and approaches to find what works best for your dog. Continuous evaluation and adaptation ensure that training remains effective, engaging, and tailored to your dog's unique characteristics and capabilities.

Dog IQ Test: Assessing Canine Intelligence

Below is an IQ test designed to assess your dog's intelligence. Please note that while this test can provide insights into your dog's cognitive abilities, it's essential to interpret the results with caution, as intelligence in dogs can manifest in various ways beyond the scope of this test. Additionally, individual differences in behavior, breed characteristics, and environmental factors can influence performance. Nevertheless, this test can serve as a fun and engaging activity to bond with your canine companion.

Dog IQ Test: Assessing Canine Intelligence

Instructions:

1. Problem-Solving Skills

- Puzzle Toy: Present your dog with a puzzle toy containing treats hidden inside. Observe how long it takes for your dog to figure out how to access the treats. Dogs that quickly solve the puzzle demonstrate higher problem-solving abilities.

2. Memory Retention

- Hide and Seek: Hide a favorite toy or treat in a designated spot while your dog watches. After a few minutes, encourage your dog to find the hidden item. Note how long it takes for your dog to locate the item and whether they remember its location from previous sessions.

3. Social Intelligence

- Name Recognition: Create a list of common household objects or family members' names. Call out the names randomly and observe whether your dog responds by looking at the named object or person. Dogs that consistently respond to their names demonstrate higher social intelligence.

4. Obedience and Training

- Basic Commands: Test your dog's response to basic commands such as sit, stay, come, and lie down. Note how quickly and accurately your dog follows each command. Dogs that respond promptly and reliably demonstrate better obedience and trainability.

5. Problem-Solving Challenges
- Obstacle Course: Set up a simple obstacle course in your backyard or living space, including hurdles, tunnels, and weave poles. Guide your dog through the course and observe how well they navigate the obstacles. Dogs that adapt quickly and overcome challenges demonstrate higher problem-solving abilities and spatial awareness.

6. Interactive Communication
- Interactive Toys: Introduce your dog to interactive toys that require manipulation or problem-solving to access treats or rewards. Observe your dog's approach to these toys and how they interact with them. Dogs that engage with interactive toys enthusiastically demonstrate curiosity and cognitive flexibility.

7. Response to Novel Stimuli
- Novel Objects: Introduce your dog to unfamiliar objects or situations, such as a new toy, novel sounds, or a strange environment. Observe your dog's reaction and how quickly they adjust to the new stimuli. Dogs that approach novel situations with curiosity and adaptability demonstrate higher intelligence.

8. Sensory Exploration
- Scent Detection Games: Set up scent detection games where your dog must locate hidden treats or objects based on their scent. Use a variety of scents and hiding spots to challenge your dog's olfactory abilities and sensory perception.

9. Imitation and Mimicry
- Copycat Games: Demonstrate a simple action or behavior, such as clapping your hands or spinning in a circle, and encourage your dog to mimic the behavior. Observe how quickly your dog picks up on the action and imitates it, reflecting their ability to learn through observation and imitation.

Scoring:
Each task can be scored on a scale from 1 to 5, with 5 indicating the highest level of performance. Total the scores from all tasks to obtain an overall assessment of your dog's intelligence.

Interpreting Results:
- While this test provides insights into your dog's cognitive abilities, remember that intelligence in dogs is multifaceted and influenced by various factors.
- Consider your dog's breed characteristics, personality traits, and individual preferences when interpreting the results.
- Use the test results as a basis for tailoring training and enrichment activities to meet your dog's specific needs and interests.

Conclusion

In the journey through the pages of this book, we've embarked on an enriching exploration of positive dog training, understanding canine behavior, mastering training principles and techniques, and prioritizing the health and wellness of our beloved companions. From laying the foundations of positive reinforcement to tailoring training programs for dogs of all ages and backgrounds, we've delved into the intricacies of building strong bonds and fostering mutual understanding between dogs and their owners.

As we conclude our journey, we're reminded of the profound impact that positive training methods can have on shaping not only a dog's behavior but also their overall well-being. By embracing empathy, patience, and compassion, we've empowered ourselves to address behavioral challenges, nurture cognitive development, and promote physical health in our canine companions.

Furthermore, the exploration of advanced training and enrichment has opened new avenues for deepening our connection with our dogs, whether through competitive sports, working roles, or therapeutic interventions. By tapping into their innate intelligence and abilities, we've unlocked the potential for collaboration, teamwork, and shared accomplishment, enriching both our lives and theirs.

As we bid farewell to these pages, let us carry forward the lessons learned and the memories shared, embracing the joy, companionship, and unconditional love that our dogs bring into our lives each day. May our continued dedication to their well-being serve as a testament to the enduring bond between humans and dogs, and may it inspire others to embark on their own journey of discovery and growth alongside their faithful companions.

With gratitude for the opportunity to embark on this journey together, we look forward to the countless adventures that await us in the company of our canine friends.

BONUS 1

HERBAL REMEDIES FOR PETS

Dear Reader,

We're thrilled to offer you our bonus "Herbal Remedies For Pets"!

Simply send an email to **laurelmarsh459@gmail.com**

with the subject line **BONUS HERBAL REMEDIES FOR PETS**, and you'll receive a PDF containing safe, effective, and natural solutions for your pet's well-being!

BONUS 2

MUSIC FOR DOG

Scan the QR code and let your dog listen to music

Dear Reader,

Your feedback is immensely valuable, not only to me but also to fellow dog owners who are considering this book. By sharing your thoughts and experiences, you're not only helping me grow as an author but also aiding others in making informed decisions about their journey in training their furry companions.

I kindly invite you to leave a review on the Amazon website. Your review can offer valuable insights and guidance to those who may benefit from the information shared in this book. Whether you found the training techniques helpful, the case studies inspiring, or have suggestions for improvement, your feedback is crucial.

Leaving a review is straightforward. Simply scan the QR code below with your mobile phone, and it will direct you straight to the review page on Amazon. Your honest review will make a significant impact, and I'm thankful for your support in spreading the message of positive training and enriching the lives of dogs and their owners.

Thank you for being a part of this journey.

Warm regards,

Laurel Marsh

Printed in Great Britain
by Amazon